SMARTER
THAN A LIE

WINNING
AGAINST LIARS WITHOUT LOSING YOUR MIND

DR. ARIN N. REEVES

Cover design by Studio02.

Copyediting by Kelli Christiansen of Bibliobibuli.

Typesetting by Quadrum Solutions Ltd.

For inquiries about bulk purchases, permission to use any of the content of this book, or speaking availability, please email info@nextions.com.

Library of Congress CIP data is on file.

ISBN:
978-1-7330647-0-5 (hardcover)
978-1-7330647-1-2 (ebook)

ZRI Publishing

Table of Contents

Section I:
Understanding the Game

Chapter 1

Section III:
Winning Against Liars …
Without Losing Your Mind

Chapter 7

Chapter 8:

Introduction

Sonia

Sonia was excited to hear that her immediate supervisor, William, had been promoted to vice president. He had been telling her for the past two years that she had worked with him that he would make sure to promote her as soon as he was promoted. William was well networked and liked by the executives of the company, and Sonia was looking forward to the ways in which her responsibilities would increase as his increased.

One day soon after his promotion, William called Sonia into his office and asked her about a complex analysis report that she had been working on for weeks. She took him through her work to that point and reminded him that, in order to finish the report, she needed him to give her the updated data that he had been responsible for gathering.

William quickly cut Sonia off and told her that he had specifically asked her to get the data, and he expressed his disappointment that she had not done so. Sonia clearly remembered the phone call during which William had said that he would pull together that information, but she didn't think it was wise to contradict him, so she apologized for any misunderstanding and told him that she would have the report done and in his inbox by the end of the day.

Sonia worked late into the evening, finished the report, and emailed it to William as she had promised. She felt like he had lied to her to get out of doing the work, but she began to wonder if she had maybe misconstrued the conversation. William had risen to the leadership ranks in a very rigorous and competitive environment. He didn't need to lie, she told herself. If he didn't want to do the work, he could have assigned it to her at any time, so he didn't need to lie about anything. She attributed the confusion to misinterpretation on her end.

When Sonia went to work the next day, she noticed that William was in his office with Andrew, the president of their division. She assumed they were discussing the report, and so she walked over to William's office to see if they had any questions about the report since she and William had not yet had a chance to discuss it.

As she neared William's office, she overheard William apologizing to Andrew for not having the report. She paused in surprise and heard William tell Andrew that he was disappointed because she—Sonia—had not completed the report. William went on to explain that he had been surprised by Sonia's lack of work ethic and commitment to the job. Andrew told William to do what he needed to do in order to, first, get the report done and, then, talk with Sonia about putting a performance plan in place to help her better understand her job requirements and expectations.

Stunned, Sonia returned to her office. She wondered if her email with the attached report had not gone through for some reason, and she chided herself for not putting a hard copy on William's desk. She checked her email outbox and tracker and saw that her email to William not only had gone through but, in fact, had been read several times during the past few hours.

As Sonia explored what had happened to her email, William appeared at her door and asked to speak with her. He entered her office, shut the door behind him, and told her that he was disappointed that she had not completed the report on time. Sonia tried to tell him that she sent him the report in an email the night before, but he interrupted her to say that he didn't receive anything from her and that he wasn't interested in her excuses. Confused and anxious, Sonia told him that she would resend the report right away. William told her not to bother because he had realized that he needed to do the report himself because she was unreliable. He also told her that he had asked Andrew to delay the meeting due to her unreliability.

Sonia was devastated after William left her office. She double-checked her outbox and made sure once again that the email had been sent correctly to William and had been registered as opened and read.

The next day, Andrew met with their team to go over the report. He began the meeting by apologizing to the team for having to delay the meeting, and he thanked William for putting in the time he needed to get the report done despite delays outside his control. Andrew did not mention Sonia's name but looked at her several times as he spoke.

As Andrew advanced to the first slide, Sonia was shocked to see her analysis—with no changes to data or presentation—on the screen. She looked at William, but he would not look in her direction. Andrew continued his presentation, and Sonia watched in confused surprise as she realized that every single slide featured the data and analysis from the report she had sent to William.

After the presentation, Andrew shook William's hand and congratulated him on a job well done. William looked at Sonia, smiled, and shrugged his shoulders.

Sonia walked back to her office and realized that William had lied to her … repeatedly. She called Kelly, one of her friends in Human Resources to tell her what happened and to ask her advice on what to do next. Kelly surreptitiously looked up Sonia's file and delivered unwelcome news to Sonia: While William had been giving her positive verbal reviews, he had filed several negative written performance reports about her, including one noting that she was "highly sensitive, incapable of taking constructive feedback, and prone to angry tantrums when confronted with errors in her work." Kelly dejectedly acknowledged to Sonia that unless she wanted to take on a visible fight with the company's leadership, she didn't have many choices other than to look for another job and leave on her own terms before she was terminated.

Sonia thought about confronting William but realized that he would probably just lie to her again. She considered going to Andrew, but, knowing that William and Andrew were friends (they socialized outside of work and their kids went to the same school), she didn't think that Andrew would believe her. She knew Kelly would help and support her if she filed an official complaint, but she also knew that Kelly was correct insofar that an official complaint would not achieve much.

Sonia talked to her family and friends about what was happening. Everyone sympathized with her, but no one offered any viable solutions, other than resigning, as to what she could do next. She didn't want to quit. She had invested several years and a lot of energy into her career, and she didn't want to lose what she had built by starting over somewhere new, especially because she would not be able to count on a recommendation from William.

Sonia continued to work at that company for several months after this incident, and she observed and experienced William's frequent lies in furtherance of his career and standing in the company. She started getting headaches on a regular basis, and several of her family and friends commented on how she wasn't her usually energetic and upbeat self.

Sonia started working for a different company about a year after the incident with William and Andrew. Although she was excited about her new job, she noticed that she was far less confident in her work than she used to be, and she was more closed off and distrusting of her coworkers than she used to be.

She knew that she was smart enough to move beyond her experiences with William. But to move forward, she knew that she needed to be smarter than the liar and the lies that had knocked her down.

Sonia was one of the first people I interviewed when I started researching liars in the workplace. I noticed how visibly upset she became when telling her story, even though it had been a couple of years since she had left her previous employer. She left the liar behind, but the pain of being lied to had stayed with her.

William engaged Sonia in a game of lies that she never consented to playing, but one that she was fooled into playing nonetheless. Once she was pulled into the game, she was trapped in the rules that William defined on William's terms. She ended up leaving the company because she didn't feel like she had any other options, but could she have stayed at the company and just walked away from William's game? Could she have played and beaten William at his game of lies without leaving the company?

Smarter Than a Lie

One of the earliest lessons we are taught in life is that it is bad to lie. Unfortunately, we are not warned that many people will ignore this lesson to their benefit and to our detriment. While many of us live by the moral code of not lying, we are not armed with the tools to deal with liars who do not live by that code.

Liars abound in every corner of our lives, but they are successful in their lying ways only if we believe their lies—that is, if we are fooled by their lies. That said, we should be gentle on ourselves for being fooled ... at least initially ... because we are wired to assume that people are telling us the truth until we have a reason to doubt them. Can you imagine what it would be like if our brains had to verify every single thing that people told us?

Our brains have three unconscious leanings that make it highly probable that we will believe liars—at least the first time they lie to us:

1. A truth bias that makes our brains default to taking in everything we hear as true—at least initially.

2. A trust bias that makes our brains default to trusting people unless we have explicit reason to not trust them.

3. An authority bias that makes our brains default to us believing that powerful people are worthy of our trust even if we have information to that contradicts what the powerful people are saying.

Liars lie, but the more we know about how liars and their lies work, the less vulnerable we can be so as not to be fooled by the lies. As humans, we can, indeed, be fooled easily, but as smart humans, we don't have to be fooled repeatedly.

Why do liars lie? Why do liars get away with lying? Why do we believe lies? Why do people enable liars even when they know they are lying? Why is it so hard to confront liars? Why is it so difficult to get over lies? How can we fight back against liars and the lies they tell? How can we win against liars?

My journeys in leadership and inclusion over the past twenty years have shown me so many ways in which people lift each other up and support each other in workplaces, but the same journeys also have opened my eyes to the many ways in which people knock others down and belittle people who don't always have the power to fight back. I have heard, noted, and analyzed hundreds of stories like Sonia's, and while the subject of liars and lying is its own field of inquiry, I have realized the extent to which liars and their lies weaken an organization's or individual's capacity to maximize the full potential for achievement, leadership, and inclusion.

As I heard more and more of these stories and dove deeper into the research about liars and their lies, I continued to be struck by how much we are taught to not to lie, but we are never taught how to deal with liars. We are armed with the moral code of truth, but we aren't given the tools to deal with those who don't live by this code. Liars are counting on us not having these tools so that they can get away with their lies.

Although I had been doing research on liars and lying for many years, Donald J. Trump's presidential campaign in 2015, eventual election in 2016, and presidential term since then brought this research to the forefront of my practice on leadership and inclusion in a way that I never could have predicted. Believe it or not, researchers who study liars and lying have incredible difficulty finding sites of research to observe liars in real life. Much of the research in this area either has been derived from carefully designed studies or extracted from the stories of people whom the liars fooled.

With President Trump, however, and for the first time in a long time, we have a real life liar lying openly in real life.

This book is not a book about, for, or against Trump. There are, though, a lot of examples featuring Trump simply because his lies are so well captured and documented through the prolific media coverage of everything he says and does. Moreover, a lot of organizations are carefully fact checking what Trump says, which means that the investigatory aspect of studying lying (i.e., the proof of a lie) has been conducted extensively by people who have dedicated enormous time and resources to this endeavor.

This book is also not about how to tell if someone is lying. Many resources (with varying degrees of reliability) focus on how to tell someone is lying. This book is about knowing what to do once you know someone is lying. In fact, the liars we will discuss lie so naturally and so frequently that the traditional "how to tell if someone is lying" information does not apply to them in the same way.

This book is about liars, the lies they tell, and the ways in which each of us can be smarter than the lies we encounter, especially in professional environments and public spaces. The ability to understand and outsmart liars in professional environments and public spaces is different than how to understand and outsmart liars in our personal lives. While much of this book can be applied to all realms, I am writing it as a resource for the worlds outside our personal lives.

As we will explore in this book, William used his position of power to lie to and about Sonia. What could Sonia have done differently to figure out what game he was playing and what mechanisms of getting away with lies he was using? What could Sonia have done to figure out what her own game was and how she could set herself up to win? We will delve into questions like this and much more in the pages ahead.

This book is *about* the Williams, the Sonias, the Andrews, and the Kellys of the world, and it's also *for* the Williams, the Sonias, the Andrews, and the Kellys of the world. I hope that the stories, research, and insights in the chapters that follow help you better understand the liars and the lies that surround us in professional and public spaces, and I hope that you learn from reading the book what I've discovered in the process of writing this book:

> Even if the liars are more powerful than us (and they often are),
> we can be smarter than the lies they tell.

Being smarter than a lie means recognizing that winning against a liar doesn't look like winning in a traditional sense. We aren't going to beat liars by outscoring them. We will beat liars by neutralizing their abilities to get in our way. We will win by rendering the liars and their lies impotent.

Being smarter than a lie means understanding that liars often might look like they are winning—and they actually might be winning for a while—but being smarter than a lie also means knowing that liars will lose in the end. The bills for their lies inevitably come due (often from unexpected sources), and when these bills come due, the liars' implosions are spectacular. Knowing this, we can play to win what we want to win regardless of what the liars are saying or doing.

It is human nature to want to focus on exposing the lies or defeating the liar or advancing the truth, but that is exactly what the liar is counting on to lure us into their traps. The second that we focus on them from the perspective of justice or vengeance, we get distracted from what we really want. Sometimes, being smarter than a lie means walking away in order to get what you want. Sometimes, it means staying and fighting. There is no right away to fight back against a liar—but there are ways that work and ways that don't work.

Ironically, the advice to walk away to win comes from Donald Trump himself: "Part of being a winner is knowing when enough is enough. Sometimes you have to give up the fight and walk away and move on to something that's more productive."[1]

Sonia could have stayed and fought back against William, but it was an equally valid strategy to walk away as well. The challenge for Sonia was that she framed walking away as quitting, as losing. Outsmarting liars means neutralizing their abilities to mess with our lives, so if walking away neutralizes them, then we have a right to frame that as a win. If walking away is not a viable or desirable option for us, then staying and playing the game to win is our right as well. The important thing is that we define winning in terms of getting what we want, not in terms of outing the liars or their lies.

Winning against a liar is about being smarter than them, and being smarter than the liars means understanding the game better, seeing the liar for whom they really are, and winning the game in a way that works for you without losing your mind in the process.

Let's get started, shall we?

Section I: Understanding the Game

RULE #1:
Recognize that all lies are not the same and that all liars are not the same.

RULE #2:
Know your brain and guard your fear.

Chapter 1:
All Lies Are Not the Same,
and All Liars Are Not the Same

I had just returned from a weekend trip out of town when my then six-year-old son, his face tight with anger, told me that he knew I had been lying to him. He reached into his pocket and pulled out a tooth, and he sighed loudly, shaking his head in disappointment. "I put this under my pillow two days ago, and I didn't tell you on purpose because I wanted to see if the Tooth Fairy was real," he said. "No Tooth Fairy, Mommy. No money. All weekend: nothing. You lied to me." My son fought my lies with facts and won. He didn't ask me to tell him the truth. He didn't get into a discussion with me. He created an experiment where the facts spoke for themselves, and that was the end of the Tooth Fairy in our home.

We all lie.

We have all lied countless times about countless things. And we will lie again many more times about many more things.

In spite of all the lessons on the morality of lies, lying is not only a natural part of being human, it also is a critical aspect of our cognitive development. The ability to create fiction, dream of futures we cannot yet see, respond to hypotheticals, and exaggerate for dramatic flair all rely on our abilities to make things up. Human beings have made things up throughout history in order to advance humanity, improve our lives, and make the world around us more enjoyable. Human beings also have made things up to get out of trouble, get what we want, persuade people to do what we want them to do, get out of doing what we don't want to do, etc. The line between creativity and deception is blurred at best. As Daniel Wallace articulates in *The Kings and Queens of Roam*, "A storyteller makes up things to help other people; a liar makes up things to help himself."[1]

According to Kang Lee, professor of Psychology at University of Toronto, children start lying when they are about two to three years old, which is about when they figure out that other people may not know what they are thinking or what they have done. About 30 percent of three-year-olds, 50 percent of four-year-olds, and 90 percent of six-year-olds lie. By the age of six, not only are children capable of creating their own lies, but their parents also have taught them how to tell white lies for social lubrication: "Tell Grandma you love the sweater she knit for you even if you hate it and never plan to wear it!"

We all lie to make our lives more livable, easier to navigate, and more fun.

However, not everyone tells the same kinds of lies. Knowing which lies to look out for is the key to understanding the game that liars are playing.

Malignant Lies Matter

People typically tell three types of lies:

- **Benevolent lies**: lies that help people, make people feel good, actively inject positivity into a negative context, etc.

    - The Lie: "Grandma, I absolutely love the sweater that you knit for me!"

    - The Fact: "I cannot stand this sweater and wish that Grandma had just given me the cash that she spent on the wool it took to make this awful sweater."

- **Benign lies**: lies that are neutral and neither help nor hurt people but allow us to navigate the world around us without creating unnecessary conflict, to be more efficient, to get things done faster, etc.

  - The Lie: "I really won't be able to make it to the event on that night. Unfortunately, I already have plans."

  - The Fact: "I really don't have any plans, but I don't want to attend your event because I have a miserable time at them, and I don't want to upset you by telling you how miserable your events are because you are a great person even if you have horrible events."

- **Malignant lies**: lies that are told by people to gain a benefit at someone else's expense, are harmful to people's lives, cause decisions to be made with false information, rely on gaslighting and other psychologically manipulative tactics, etc.

  - The Lie: "Are you sure you aren't confused about what happened? I never said what you think I said."

  - The Fact: "I know you are not confused, and I know that you are telling the truth, but it would suit me better if I can convince you that you are confused and screwed up so that I don't have to take responsibility for what I did wrong. Besides, who are you going to complain to, anyway?"

The framework of benevolent (helpful), benign (not harmful), and malignant (harmful) allows us to understand lies through the various facets of what each lie was, why the liar lied, and how the lie affected the person to whom it was told.

Most of us tell benevolent and benign lies—i.e., lies that generally are anchored to facts, traditions, or our own opinions. My son was not happy about the benevolent (some may argue benign) lies I had told him about the Tooth Fairy, but those lies were rooted in a cultural tradition that allowed him to understand I was not trying to hurt him with the lie.

When I initially began researching liars and lying, I became (and have stayed) uncomfortably conscious of how often I lie. In 2017, I challenged myself to keep a journal of the lies I told over a five-day period. It turns out that I lie on average of about two times a day when I'm not around a lot of people and about four times a day when I network, work with clients, and/or socialize with family and friends.

My lies during those five days were mostly benign lies that included: telling people I was not tired when I was exhausted, telling an airline representative that I had an emergency at home (which I did not) to try to get on an earlier flight back to Chicago, telling a relative that I had a conference call waiting (which I did not) to get off the phone with them, telling a friend that I had plans (which I did not) to avoid going to a dinner, and saying I was not sore after working out (I was very sore) because I wanted to appear more fit than I was. I also frequently minimized how much time I had spent on Twitter (by about a third), and I exaggerated how much time I had spent looking over some documents I had not wanted to review. I also told a few other lies that I don't want to share here (hey, even researchers get some privacy!).

The above don't include the benevolent lies I told myself in order to get through a moment, and event or a day (e.g., "This will be worth it in the long run" when I knew it wouldn't be or "It's not as bad as it seems" when it was exactly as bad as it seemed). I also had some "fake it till you make it" justifications to keep myself going, and I broke several promises I made to myself (although, technically, I'm not sure if breaking promises is lying).

I took my full list of lies to an industrial psychologist who also is an expert in liars and lying and asked her to analyze me as a liar. I awaited a diagnosis of "Oh, my goodness, how could you lie so much!" but got a "You are an average liar whose lies are primarily harmless lies used for social lubrication and motivational emotional management purposes." According to the psychologist, I mostly lie to other people to avoid unnecessary social friction and even some normal social conversations (I'm an introvert), and I lie to myself to motivate myself and keep going when the going gets tough (I'm an overachiever).

I fully admit (because I would not want to lie here!) that these lies do not fully capture all the lies I've told in my life. There have been many, some of which I would repeat if pushed and some of which I would not, but upon reflection, I do realize that the psychologist had me accurately pegged. I lie to get out of having to do stuff with people without hurting their feelings, and I lie to trick myself into forging forward with goals when I'm tired or feeling defeated. Overall, I'm pretty average when it comes to lying.

As it turns out, most of us are pretty average when it comes to lying. We lie regularly, but we tell mostly benevolent or benign lies to maintain social norms and traditions, get out of uncomfortable situations, and preserve others' or our own feelings.

Benevolent and benign lies, often in the shape of white lies and half-truths, are told proactively to help others or defensively out of fear (e.g., of causing conflict, of offending, of being vulnerable, of getting hurt, of hurting someone, of revealing insecurities, of angering someone). The benevolent lies we tell make others feel good, and the benign lies we tell protect ourselves and/or others from something unpleasant.

Malignant lies, on the other hand, are told to help the malignant liar and only the malignant liar. Malignant liars are focused on helping themselves regardless of the pain inflicted on others. Thus, most liars who tell malignant lies are not creative, original, or sporadic in how they lie. Malignant liars are rote, predictable, and consistently unrelenting in shaping their realities by misshaping everyone else's.

Beware of Malignant Liars

Malignant liars spew self-serving lies—i.e., lies that help them get what they want, avoid what they don't want, blame someone else when things go wrong, feel better about themselves at someone else's expense, and break any and all rules that stand in their way. They lie to deceive and manipulate others in order to achieve their self-centered needs. They tell self-serving and sometimes cruel lies, not to ward off or smooth over anything, but to create fake realities where they can manipulate people into getting what they want no matter how much it hurts someone else.

The moral anchors of benevolent and benign liars, unlike those of malignant liars, are moored to the truth as the right thing to do even as we strain against that anchor from time to time for myriad reasons. However, when we strain, we feel the strain. We feel the pull of the anchor. Lying takes effort on our parts, and it takes a toll on us. We may be worried about the lie being discovered, or we may feel guilty about getting away with it. Average liars may feel the strain to various extents, but we do feel the strain. We know that we lied, and we feel bad about it, albeit to varying degrees.

Malignant liars do not feel the strain. They are not—nor do they care to be—moored to the truth, so they don't feel a strain when they pull away from it. For malignant liars, both truths and lies are stories that are available equally to them on the same menu, and they can choose what they want in that moment based on what they want to achieve. They don't fear getting caught because, in their minds, there is nothing to catch. Psychiatry, neurology, and psychology have a long way to go before we can fully understand all the machinations of malignant liars, but we do know that these liars also tend to be self-centered, selfish, insecure, abusive, obsessive, controlling, impulsive, aggressive, jealous, manipulative, socially uncomfortable, emotionally volatile, vindictive, lack empathy, and/or quick to anger.

Malignant liars do not feel the same repulsion to lying as average liars do. They lie to get what they want, and they see their words as strategic, not deceptive. They think in terms of efficiency, not right or wrong. A 2014 study titled *A Few Prolific Liars: Variation in the Prevalence of Lying*[2] gives us a general profile of malignant liars. They:

- tell almost six white lies to every one told by an average person, and they tell almost twenty big lies (malignant lies) to every one big lie told by an average person;

- are far more likely than the average person to lie for their own self-interest (e.g., getting what they want, protecting a secret that could hurt them), and they are far less likely than the average person to lie to protect other people; and

- are more likely to be men who are in higher levels of occupational power.

Workplaces are teeming with liars, but the majority of liars in workplaces are benign liars who lie to defend themselves. The malignant liars are fewer in number, but we know that they are primarily men. Indeed, the greatest concentration of malignant liars in workplace is among men in positions of power. Moreover, the people whom these malignant liars are most likely to lie to are women, usually women who rank lower than them in their organization's hierarchy.

For malignant liars, self-serving lying is a routine part of life that gives them comfort, security, the spoils they are seeking, and even a sense of peace. Lying to others to feel more secure doesn't feel like a good strategy for most of us because we would worry about getting caught, and that would feel worse for us in the long run. For malignant liars, though, lying to others to feel secure makes perfect sense because getting caught doesn't mean anything. They don't necessarily need you to believe them. If they can get away with lying long enough to get what they want, they consider their efforts successful.

Dr. Bella DePaulo, Academic Affiliate in Psychological & Brain Sciences at University of California Santa Barbara, has studied liars and lying extensively, and she has specifically studied the most insidious of lies: cruel lies. Cruel lies are those "that hurt of disparage or embarrass or belittle other people" to the point of incredible personal and/or professional devastation. She found that while 1 to 2 percent of average people's lies tend to be cruel lies, 40 to 50 percent of malignant liars' lies are cruel lies.

Given the tendencies of malignant liars to lie in cruel and self-serving ways, it may seem like they would be shunned and rejected by average people. Unfortunately, malignant liars are excellent at lying. According to researchers who study the science and art of lie detection, most of us are generally terrible at knowing when we are being lied to,[3] and a significant part of why we fall for the lies of malignant liars (at least initially) is because they have a unique combination of skills that makes us believe them. By nature or nurture, malignant liars are:

- Physically attractive by general social standards,

- Intelligent and quick on their feet,

- Manipulative in a relaxed and confident way,

- Talented performers who love having an audience,

- Eloquent speakers and animated conversationalists,

- Emotionally deceptive by actively hiding their true feelings,

- Able to answer questions in unverifiable ways and to provide information in measured doses in order to make sure that no one knows enough at any one time, and

- Excellent at reading people and changing their *modus operandi* quickly in response to changes in others.[4]

Malignant liars are exactly the type of people—attractive, intelligent, confident, eloquent—we are socialized to believe, and they are exactly the type of people who saunter into positions of success and leadership. Once these liars attract us into their webs, they can manipulate us to get what they want. If we are fortunate enough to see through the manipulation and get out of their webs, we see the facts for what they are—even if we also realize that we don't have recourse to undo what they have done (at least not on our own). Unfortunately, for every person who manages to escape a malignant liar's web, there are dozens of believers still trapped in that web.

We cannot fight back against malignant liars by calling them liars or pointing out truths that counter their lies because their lies can be interpreted as truth (by themselves and their believers) even if they are not rooted in fact. Their lying is rooted in creating an imagined world for themselves and others in which the liar is dominant, secure, and idolized. Fighting the liars by shouting that they are lying only signals to them that we are paying attention, choosing to spend our time, energy, and resources on them, all of which only strengthens the truth of their imaginary worlds.

Malignant liars are better than most of us at lying. Malignant liars are so good at lying and manipulating us with lies that they can become quite powerful. They can fool global stock markets. They can control Hollywood. They can even become President of the United States.

The Malignant Liar's Persuasion versus Manipulation Trick
L'heure entre chien et loup

The literal translation of the French idiom above is "hour between dog and wolf," which signifies the time immediately after the sun sets but before the sky becomes completely dark. In the "hour between the dog and wolf, there is still enough light for us to see the world around us, but all that is seen is filtered through the haze of dusk. What once was clear is now ambiguous. In this hour, we cannot discern the difference between a dog (a friend) or a wolf (foe). We cannot distinguish between safety and danger."

Persuasion and manipulation are the identical apparitions of the dog and wolf, respectively, and being human means that we are always trying to discern between persuasion and manipulation in sometimes hazy interactions with others.

Persuasion is a friend to be attracted.

It is a necessary skill to navigate and succeed in any social network. As members of a family, a community, an organization, a nation, or any other group of people, when we need others to listen to us, love us, meet our needs, help us when we need assistance, etc., we must persuade them to do so. Persuasion allows us to coexist and connect with others in ways that enhance our lives as well as theirs. Moreover, it can be fun to be persuaded to try new things, enjoy new adventures, and take calculated risks that push us out of our comfort zones.

Persuasion, however, has a dangerous doppelganger—manipulation—which looks and sounds a lot like persuasion but results in a degradation of our lives for someone else's benefits.

11

Manipulation is a danger to be avoided.

To distinguish persuasion from manipulation, we have to dissect "the intent behind the desire to persuade, the truthfulness and transparency of the process, and the net benefit or impact on the person being persuaded."[5] Manipulation is persuasion, but it "implies persuasion with the intent to fool, control or contrive the person on the other side of the conversation into doing something, believing something, or buying into something that leaves them either harmed or without benefit."[6]

Persuasion is based on facts. Manipulation is based on malignant lies.

Malignant Liars in Action

Houston, Texas (2001)
The Rise and Fall of Enron

For six years in a row, from 1995 to 2000, Enron was applauded as the most innovative company by *Fortune* Magazine's Most Admired Companies survey. It also was consistently the highest-ranking global energy company on *Fortune*'s 100 Best Companies to Work for in America. It was one of the hottest trading stocks in the stock market, and it attracted the best and brightest talent from all over the world. It was a shining star among superstar companies. In 2000, Enron had revenues of $111 billion and employed more than twenty thousand people.

In 2001, the shine faded. Between August 2000 and November 2001, Enron's stock price plummeted from $90.75 to $0.26. While the stock price was plummeting, Enron's founder, chairman, and CEO, Kenneth Lay, promised his employees that the company was on the brink of a turnaround and encouraged them to buy more stock—while he and other executives were dumping their own shares as fast as they could.

On December 2, 2001, Enron filed for bankruptcy. Its collapse cost investors more than $60 billion, destroyed thousands of jobs, and lost employees over $2 billion in their pension plans.

It may have ended up being one of the greatest corporate tragedies in our country, but it became one of the biggest corporate scandals instead. Why? Lies.

When Mark Koenig, Enron's former head of investor relations, testified in the criminal trials that followed the fall of Enron, he admitted that he had frequently lied about revenues and other financial information to investors and analysts who relied on his statements—all at the unsaid nudging of Lay and of Jeffrey Skilling, Enron's CEO at the time. Koenig pled guilty to aiding and abetting securities fraud and cooperated with the prosecution for a reduced sentence in prison.

Enron's Lie: "We say we are making more money than we are really making, and we are losing less money than we say we are losing."

The lie worked for more than a decade. When it started unraveling in 2001, we all learned just how prolific the liars involved really were. Enron's core business was buying and selling energy through financial instruments in equity markets, an incredibly innovative idea at that time. They expanded into creating and selling other assets, such as advertisement time on television and insurance risk in the form of derivatives through dozens of trading ventures, some of which succeeded but many of which failed. They could have been honest about their losses, learned from them and moved on. Instead, they chose to lie.

The fabricated reality that Enron created was that they were such a profitable and innovative company that if you didn't understand their methods, it wasn't because they were lying, it was because you were too mired in conventional business models to understand their shiny new innovative ways. Kenneth Lay, Jeffrey Skilling, and Andrew Fastow, the three most senior executives at Enron, lied so much, so quickly, and so frequently, that it took years to unravel and understand exactly what happened. Lay, the founder and mastermind behind Enron, was the company's CEO when it was formed in 1985; Lay hired Skilling in 1990 to keep Wall Street happy and to keep Enron innovating in deregulated markets; Lay hired Fastow the same year to take care of the finance and accounting functions in innovative new ways.

All three of them knew that Enron was not the profitable company that Wall Street thought it was, so their business strategies were not focused on creating a stronger company. Instead, they were focused on hiding what a weak company it really was. Fastow created financial structures that were so complex and convoluted that Enron was able to hide the truth about their finances under the cover of complexity. Enron's accountants and auditors, Arthur Andersen, were pulled in by the riptide of lies and went down with Enron when the lies were brought to light.

Let's take a quick journey through one of Enron's elaborate lies. In 2000, Enron made a deal with Blockbuster Video that they estimated to be worth about $110 million. They inked the deal and borrowed money from a Canadian bank based on market evaluations of Enron's worth, which we now know was based on lies. The business failed miserably, and Blockbuster got out of the contract, but Enron continued to list profits from this deal because they were using shell companies to funnel money from the bank loan into Enron as revenue.

The number of malignant lies that Lay, Skilling, and others needed to tell for more than a decade could be described as nothing short of prolific. The charge of insider trading—when they were selling their Enron shares while encouraging employees to buy more shares—is where these malignant liars showed their truest and most malignant selves. They used their employees' fears of financial ruin and their employees' trust in them as leaders to mitigate their losses even though they knew that their employees' financial lives would be devastated as a result.

Lay, Skilling, and Fastow are illustrative profiles in malignant lying. They lied to get what they wanted, lied to cover up their lies, and lied to try to make others take the fall for their lies. Their lies were so loud that the facts couldn't be heard for years.

Hollywood (2017)
#MeToo

Most malignant liars lie directly, but malignant liars also can lie in indirect ways through the targeted uses of power and control that broadcast a lie so loudly that the facts cannot break through.

In October 2017, *The New York Times* ran a story about how Harvey Weinstein had been sexually harassing and assaulting women for decades and had evaded all consequences for his behavior through denials, threats, and confidential settlements with strict nondisclosure clauses. Weinstein, the name behind some of the entertainment industry's biggest hits including movies, such as *Sex, Lies, and Videotape*; *Pulp Fiction*; and *Good Will Hunting*, and television shows such as *Project Runway*, had preyed upon dozens of women who worked and aspired to work in the entertainment industry, where he was one of the biggest financiers, decision makers, and influencers.

The fact is that there are laws to protect each of us from unwanted physical contact from another person, and these laws are supposed to govern how we interact with each other in society generally and in workplaces specifically. Malignant liars not only disregard facts like this, but they also put systems in place to protect themselves when they circumvent the facts to get what they want. As Megan Twohey, one of the two reporters who broke the Weinstein story in *The New York Times*, said:

> [T]here were these fears that to speak out against Weinstein in any way could have negative repercussions for people's career paths. Just because people had left the Weinstein Co. or Miramax didn't mean that they felt that they were clear of Harvey Weinstein. This was a man whose tentacles extended to basically all areas of the entertainment industry. "Gatekeeper" is a great way to describe the role that Harvey played in the industry. Young assistants who worked for him were told if you pay your dues and go through this intense boot camp, in which you may have to suffer abuse, you will be rewarded. A letter of recommendation from Harvey Weinstein will open doors to get

you the jobs that you dream of getting some day. By the same token, if you speak out, those pathways will close down.[7]

The abuse that women who worked for Weinstein had to endure included being forced to massage him while he was naked, watch him shower, watch him masturbate, and engage in sexual contact and intercourse with him in exchange for a promise that he would not actively destroy their careers. The threat against career destruction was conveniently coupled with the potential promise of career opportunities for the women's compliance.

Harvey Weinstein's Lie: "The laws that grant you autonomy over your body and the freedom from a hostile work environment don't apply to me, so you either do what I ask, or you suffer the consequences of doors in the entertainment industry slamming in your face."

Under the cover of oppressive nondisclosure agreements, confidential multimillion-dollar settlements when he pushed women too far, and the complicit silence of many in the industry who knew what was going on, Weinstein's lie that the laws didn't apply to him reverberated loudly through the entertainment industry's culture and appeared to be the truth because he was never held accountable for his actions.

Given the success of his previous lies, it was no surprise that, when *The New York Times* article broke through Weinstein's malignant lie in October 2017, Weinstein tried to lie his way out of the facts. But the article had broken the silence, and the facts flooded the news with stories from almost a hundred women, including household names like Ashley Judd, Angelina Jolie, Selma Hayek, Gwyneth Paltrow, and Lupita Nyong'o.[8] The facts grew loud enough to explode the nascent #MeToo movement into popular culture, get Weinstein fired from the company he founded, and result in criminal sexual assault charges against the man who lived his life in the lie that he was above the law.

In his first interview after *The New York Times* exposé, Weinstein, without irony, stated that, "What I am saying is that I bear responsibility for my actions, but the reason I am suing is because of the *Times*' inability to be honest with me, and their reckless reporting. They told me lies."[9]

New York (2015)
Trump University

In late 2004, economists were starting to whisper about a coming downturn in the U.S. and global economies:

> Current conditions show weakening economic growth and labor market … Growth is slowing, because the job market remains weak, real wages and incomes continue to fall, and energy prices have risen sharply. The worst trade and current account deficits in U.S. history also threaten a potential dollar crisis that would drive up interest rates and further slow the economy. With the United States and China weakening, another sustained jump in oil prices could trigger a global downturn in 2005.[10]

The housing market also started cooling in 2004 after years of robust expansion. As with any major economic and financial crises, individual fears of loss of autonomy, separation, and loss/death of ego increase as people worry about themselves and their families.

Against the backdrop of a financially vulnerable period in the American economy, falling incomes, and a rapidly deteriorating housing market, Donald Trump, Michael Sexton, and Jonathan Spitalny introduced a new for-profit educational company called Trump University. Donald Trump, the *de facto* owner with 93 percent ownership interest in Trump University, was the face and voice of the venture, selling the company's offerings in real estate, asset management, entrepreneurship, and wealth creation. The primary sales pitch was that if you paid to attend Trump University's seminars, you could be like Donald Trump.

The infomercials and advertisements for Trump University featured Trump making statements such as "At Trump University, we teach success … Success … it's going to happen to you … Trump University is about how to become successful" while a narrator tells the viewer that "Donald Trump, without question, is the world's most famous businessman." Trump asserted that he could "turn anyone into a successful real estate investor." Trump convinced people to part with the limited resources they had in order to chase the dream of being like Trump, of possibly never having to worry about running out of resources ever again.

Trump promised that the "professors and adjunct professors ... are absolutely terrific ... best of the best ... these are all the people who are handpicked by me ... we're going to teach you about business better than the best business schools, and I went to the best business school."

Trump's Trump University Lie: "Signing up for Trump University made you successful, and if it wasn't working, it wasn't Trump University, it was you ... because Donald Trump said so."

In its five years of existence, Trump made about $5 million through tuition paid by 6,698 students who attended a three-day seminar at $1,495 per seminar or upgraded to mentoring programs that cost up to $35,000 per year. Students were convinced to shell out these high fees thanks to Trump's assertion that he was the "most famous businessman," that the instructors were "people who are handpicked," and that Trump University was "better than the best business schools." Because many of these students wanted to see themselves as successful, the guarantee of success from someone who looked like he had achieved success triggered the consistency urge: If they didn't take these courses, how would they ever end up as rich and successful as Trump? If they didn't attend Trump University, were they not committed to being successful?

The students liked Trump, and he touted high ratings from more than 90 percent of the people who had attended Trump University, which provided the consensus potential students needed to transition them to registration. The overwhelming majority of the students were in financially vulnerable situations, but they were convinced to use their limited financial resources to sign up for Trump University.

The State of New York charged Trump with lying about being a university because it was not a university and did not do anything that a university needed to do to earn the title. Roughly 38 percent of Trump University students—2,539 of the 6,698—demanded and received refunds because the courses were built on lies and didn't provide anything they were supposed to.

Other states and dozens of individuals filed lawsuits accusing Trump University of "not just of fraud, false advertising, and unfair business practices, but also of having used such tactics against vulnerable seniors in ways that violated special 'financial elder abuse' statutes in California and Florida."[11] In depositions for the suits, Trump admitted that he was not at all involved in the selection of any of the instructors that he had promised were handpicked by him. Investigations further revealed that Trump was not at all involved in creating any of the curricula that had promised to reveal Trump's investing secrets. Some of the curricula were even revealed to be fully plagiarized imitations of generic business investing texts available in bookstores. Basically, the whole thing was one big loud lie made up of a lot of little lies.

As this evidence bubbled to the surface during the 2016 presidential election cycle, Trump called the people suing him liars. He attacked the federal judge assigned to his case, Judge Gonzalo P. Curiel, as being biased because Judge Curiel was a Mexican American. He told the American people that he would never settle because he was right and because everyone suing him was wrong. After all the puffery, for a business that made him less than $5 million, Trump settled the lawsuits collectively for $25 million.

Trump did what every malignant liar always does: When confronted by his malignant lies, he told even more malignant lies.

And, then he settled—after the presidential election.

Jim

A few years ago, I was working with an organization whose CEO, Jim, turned out to be a malignant liar. On the surface, he was charming and attentive, and he seemed to be exactly the type of client that we love to partner with for research and consulting projects.

Within a few weeks of working with him, however, we realized that Jim did not like to do any work, but he was keen on appearing like he did a lot of work. These were incompatible goals, and he lied, prolifically, to bridge the gap.

He lied every time we interacted with him and in ways that truly bewildered my team and me. During our scheduled calls with preapproved (by him!) agendas, Jim would ignore the agenda and bring up topics that he falsely claimed we had asked him to discuss. He lied about not sending emails he did send and wouldn't acknowledge the emails when we forwarded him what he sent us as proof. He asked us to create proposals for projects and then would deny that he asked us to do so after we sent him the detailed proposals.

We tried working with someone else on his team as an intermediary, but we quickly realized that this person only justified and enabled Jim's lies. We couldn't tell whether she believed the lies, but she definitely stood by the lies and acted as if they were not lies.

My team and I became so paranoid and anxious whenever we talked with Jim or anyone on his team that we assigned someone on our team to be on each call to do nothing but take notes. We summarized everything in emails to make sure we were all on the same page, but he would never respond to us. Sure enough, the next time we spoke, he would tell us that he never asked us to do what he asked us to do. He asked us to help him on projects that had nothing to do with our contract or skill sets. He once asked me to plan an event for him, and if you know anything about me, you know that I am indeed the last person on Earth that you would want to plan an event! When we told him that we couldn't do that, he told us we were unhelpful and terrible at client service.

He lied to us about conversations that he said he had with other clients of ours. When we checked in with our clients, they told us completely different stories about the conversations. He told some people that he and I were getting to be really good friends, and he told others that he believed me to have a temper problem. Neither was true, although the situation was making the latter much more of a realistic probability than it ever had been in my life.

This went on for several months, during which we were unable to move forward on several of the projects we were supposed to deliver for Jim and his organization. He wouldn't give us the approvals we needed to move forward, and then he would berate us for not making progress. When we would ask him about the approvals, he would ignore the countless emails and voicemails from us and then call us and ask why we were delayed with our deliverables. One person on the team would cry after our calls with him. Another person (okay, me) would ready a drink before a call with him because I knew I would need one after speaking with him.

We were living in a fabricated reality that Jim had created in which he capitalized on my team's fears of doing substandard work, disappointing a client, and harming our reputation for excellence in both work product and client service. We were trapped in Jim's lies, and even though we knew they were lies, we didn't know how to get out of this world he had created.

Our firm has always operated on the fundamentals of joy, kindness, and excellence, as well as for continuous improvement, innovative problem solving, and leading for impact. We hold each other accountable for living these values in everything we do internally with the firm and externally with our clients and other constituents. We were devastated by what was happening with this client, so much so that I engaged an industrial psychologist to assess what was going on and help us find a way out, around, or through the mess.

While the psychologist was assessing the situation, Jim called me and asked if I could meet him for lunch because he was concerned about the work that we were doing for them and wanted to talk about contract renewals. Over lunch, he proceeded to tell me how disappointed he was that we hadn't delivered anything that he had asked us to deliver. My team and I had prepared for this possibility, and I was armed with a folder with all the email exchanges, timelines for all the projects, and approvals we were waiting for from him before we could move forward.

I opened the folder to go through the specifics with him when he reached over to me, closed the folder, and said, "Arin, those emails aren't the issue. The issue is that you are just not doing what you are contracted to do."

Jim's "truth" was that we weren't doing what we were contracted to do. The "fact" was that we weren't being given the chance to do what we were contracted to do.

I reopened the folder to point out how my team and I literally had been blocked by him in doing the work that he was criticizing us for not doing, when he reached over and shut the folder again. This time, he said, "Sweetheart, you really aren't hearing me."

I froze. "Sweetheart?" I looked at him, fought back the urge to slap him, picked up my folder, and left without saying a word.

After processing the event with my team and the psychologist, we realized that the lying was a strategy to create a scapegoat for why key projects at the organization had not even been started, let alone completed.

I called one of the directors to whom Jim reported, and I shared with him the facts on all that had been happening and my concerns about Jim's behavior. I shared the emails, the notes from our calls, our detailed timelines, and all other communications between my team and the organization. The director did not sound surprised by what I was saying, but he was surprised by the mountain of information I had sent him. He assured me that no one on the Board of Directors would ever believe that we had been negligent in doing the work we were hired to do. He offered to play a role in renegotiating the contract. I told him I would get back to him.

I met with the psychologist and asked for her advice about how to proceed. She took me through her assessment, and her simple and unwavering conclusion was that we needed to fire this client.

She told me that we were dealing with a person who didn't have the same relationship with facts that most people have. "So, he's a liar," I repeated. "It's not that simple," she told me.

Jim had created a fake world in which we were constantly blocked from moving forward, and he preyed on the relentless commitment that my team and I have, both for not quitting and for completing projects for our clients at any cost. He focused on his "truth" that we weren't doing the work we needed to do, and we focused on our "truth" that we were doing our best. This battle of truths has no winner.

The fact was that there was no figuring out how to work with Jim because he had no intention of working with us. The real solution out of this fake world was to stay focused on the facts, share the facts with Jim's bosses, fire Jim as a client, and learn the lesson that it is impossible to work with a malignant liar.

We fired Jim. He yelled and cursed at us. He told us we would regret it and that he would make sure that no one ever worked with us again. The psychologist had prepared us for this. We stayed focused on the facts and didn't respond to his threats. We told him that we wished him the best, and we hung up the phone feeling lighter than we had in months. The organization's Board of Directors fired Jim a few months after we dropped them as a client.

We debriefed with the psychologist about what we had experienced during the many months that we had worked with this person, and we had a party to celebrate the end of "the craziness," as we referred to it.

I haven't spoken to Jim since we fired him, and I still shudder when I think about what my team and I went through for months because of him. But I am grateful to Jim because our experiences with him led to an intellectual curiosity about liars and lying that has become one of our core research areas.

The Players Aren't Always Individual People

Most malignant liars appear to be charming and intelligent people, and this makes it easier for them to persuade people to think, say, and do what they want them to do. However, real persuaders rely on facts; beneath the manipulator's veneer of persuasion lies a dense bedrock of lies.

What Lay, Skilling, Weinstein, and Trump have in common is that they were all viewed as charismatic and brilliant persuaders. What they also had in common is that beneath their persuasive veneers were malignant lies designed to convince people to do things that were harmful to themselves while benefitting the liar. Hiding behind their charismatic façades, they used their malignant lies to prevent the facts from ruining their plans for as long as they could.

These men were the leaders who guided their organizations, but manipulation rooted in malignant lies isn't utilized only by individuals and the companies they run: Entire industries can engage in malignant lies that look like persuasion on the surface but are insidiously manipulative, designed to benefit the industry's monetary interests despite the harms caused to the customers and other constituents.

Just What the Doctor Ordered

By the early 1950s, scientific evidence had started accumulating that smoking cigarettes contributed to, if not caused, lung cancer. Internally, tobacco companies accepted this, but they also realized the potential for financial ruin if they externally admitted it. So they hired a public relations company, Hill and Knowlton, in 1953.[12] Hill and Knowlton quickly assessed the situation and understood their job to be to "Stop public panic … free millions of Americans from the guilty fear that is going to arise deep in their biological depths—regardless of any pooh-poohing logic—every time they light a cigarette."[13]

Hill and Knowlton understood that the emerging scientific evidence pointing to a link between smoking and lung cancer would scare cigarette smokers into not smoking, and they determined that the only way that tobacco companies could continue to make money was to manipulate the general public into believing that the scientific evidence was not what it was.

In 1954, the U.S. tobacco industry issued a statement titled "Frank Statement to Cigarette Smokers" (we'll get to this later in the book, but anytime someone says, "let me be honest" or "let me be frank," "trust me," or "believe me" … chances are good that they are lying). The statement argued that:

"Distinguished authorities point out:

- That medical research of recent years indicates many potential causes of lung cancer.

- That there is no agreement among the authorities regarding what the cause is.

- That there is no proof that cigarette smoking is one of the causes.

- That statistics purporting to link smoking with the disease could apply with equal force to any one of many other aspects of modern life. Indeed, the validity of the statistics themselves are questioned by numerous scientists."[14]

Tobacco industry scientists met with industry executives and determined that it was common knowledge among executives in these companies that smoking caused lung cancer. The public message, however, from the tobacco companies was that "in our considered opinion there is no proof at all that smoking causes lung cancer and much to suggest that it cannot be the cause."[15] The scientific evidence mounted, and the U.S. Surgeon General concluded in 1964 that "cigarette smoking is causally related to lung cancer in men; the magnitude of the effect of cigarette smoking far outweighs all other factors." The tobacco companies responded with "We don't accept the idea that there are harmful agents in tobacco."

More research found that smoking causes cancer. Tobacco companies responded with statements such as "none of the things which have been found in tobacco smoke are at concentrations which can be considered harmful. Anything can be considered harmful. Applesauce is harmful if you get too much of it."

This back and forth continued for decades until whistleblowers, lawsuits, public information campaigns, and other efforts shut down the Hill and Knowlton PR madness and got tobacco companies to admit that they lied. Tobacco companies got away with blatant lies for fifty years in the United States (they have now taken the lies to developing countries) through Hill and Knowlton's strategy to deal with the science linking smoking to lung cancer: "(a) smearing or belittling them; (b) trying to overwhelm them with mass publication of the opposed viewpoints of other specialties; (c) debating them in the public arena; or (d) raise the issue far above them ... and then we can make our case."[16]

Although tobacco companies have not fully taken responsibility for maintaining their lies as long as they did, their journey gives us a peek into how organizations and even entire industries can manipulate with malignant lies ... for decades.

Smarter Than the Lies

For all intents and purposes, these liars (individuals, organizations, or industries) look like master persuaders on the surface, but persuasion is persuasion only when it is based in facts. When persuasion is rooted in lies, it is no longer persuasion. It becomes manipulation. And, those who excel at manipulation become malignant liars.

Malignant liars are so good that it's often difficult to spot the lies they are telling and the fake realities they are weaving until it's too late. It's harder still to understand why some people might continue to believe these liars' lies even when the lies are clearly disproven. It's most difficult to fight back against these liars' malignant manipulations, especially when these manipulations threaten how we live in and navigate the world around us.

Fighting back against these lies requires being smarter than the lies in a way that allows us to drown the lies out with facts.

If you ask people to identify the opposite of a lie, almost everyone will say that a truth is the opposite of a lie. This is not only incorrect, it also is the first thing that malignant liars count on when they think about how to trap us in their malignant lies. Facts are proven. Truths are believed. Malignant liars count on people believing a possible truth in order to mask facts that are incorrect and can be proven so.

The opposite of a lie is not a truth. The opposite of a lie is a fact.

Fighting Back With Facts

We can learn about malignant liars by studying Ken Lay, Jeff Skilling, Harvey Weinstein, Donald Trump, and the tobacco industry, but we can learn about how to win against these liars by studying Sherron Watkins, Lauren O'Connor, Tarla Makaeff, and Jeffrey Wigand. You may have never heard of these people, but each, in his or her own way, found a way to be smarter than the malignant liars who took advantage of them.

Sherron Watkins was vice president of corporate development at Enron. When she wrote a memo laying out the facts about the financial and accounting irregularities at Enron and got nowhere with Lay and other executives, she released her memo to the authorities. Her actions marked the beginning of the end for Enron and earned her a Person of the Year nod in 2002 from *TIME Magazine* for being a courageous whistleblower.

Lauren O'Connor used to work with Harvey Weinstein at the Weinstein Company. She wrote a memo detailing dates, times, and incidents about her interactions with and observations of Weinstein to the executives at the company about the "toxic environment for women" and expressed her concern that Weinstein was using female employees like her to provide cover for his lies to "vulnerable women who hope he will get them work." Weinstein lied and called her accusations baseless. O'Connor persisted and continued to pressure the company's Board of Directors and other executives to pay attention. As she stated in her memo, "I am a 28-year-old woman trying to make a living and a career. Harvey Weinstein is a 64-year-old, world famous man and this is his company. The balance of power is me: 0, Harvey Weinstein: 10." It was that memo that prevented Weinstein from being able to hide after *The New York Times* article was published, and it was that memo that got him fired from his eponymous company.

Tarla Makaeff was one of the first people to sue Trump University. She endured scathing personal attacks from Donald Trump and his attorneys for years, but she racked up several legal victories between 2010 and 2015, which paved the way for subsequent lawsuits to achieve their eventual success. One of Trump's primary attacks on Makaeff was that she was complimentary of Trump University when she was a student and agreed to vocalize her praise in a promotional video for the organization. Makaeff persisted in her efforts to bring Trump's deceptive practices to light, and the court ruled in her favor, saying "as the recent Ponzi-scheme scandals involving onetime financial luminaries like Bernard Madoff and Allen Stanford demonstrate, victims of con artists often sing the praises of their victimizers until the moment they realize they have been fleeced."[17]

Jeffrey Wigand was a chemist who had been an employee at one of the country's iconic tobacco companies, Brown & Williamson. In 1995, Wigand broke his confidentiality agreement and testified against tobacco companies in a case in Mississippi in which he asserted that tobacco companies had been manipulating nicotine content, lying about the dangerous addictive properties of nicotine, and thwarting efforts to create safer, healthier cigarettes. Wigand's testimony was covered by *The Wall Street Journal*, and he agreed to an interview on *60 Minutes*, during which he made all the information about the tobacco industry's lies available to the general public. Wigand's decision to speak out—at great peril to himself and his family—marked the beginning of the end of the *modus operandi* of tobacco companies and highlighted their liability to the thousands of people who literally were sickened to death by their lies.

As with these well-known whistleblowers, my team and I were smarter than Jim's lies because we played his game with facts. We documented the facts, kept track of the facts, and communicated the facts in a cohesive and comprehensive way so that we could express the reality to the people who could and did (eventually) hold Jim accountable. We never called him a liar (although we really wanted to), and we never argued with him because arguing legitimized his story. We ignored his story and told ours with facts.

Sherron Watkins, Lauren O'Connor, Tarla Makaeff, and Jeffrey Wigant (and my own team) went up against some manipulative liars who told extremely malignant lies, but each of them (and us) found a way to be heard above the lies—with courage, persistence, and facts.

Distinguishing lies from truths is difficult. Separating lies from facts is much easier as Watkins, O'Connor, Makaeff, and Wigand proved.

Technically, when executives at Enron were posting incoming funds from shell companies, a truth was that there was money coming in. But the provable fact was that the money coming in was not revenue from any goods or services sold. It was incoming money, but it was not revenue.

Weinstein had never been disciplined, fired, or arrested for his abusive behavior with women, so it was easy for people to believe that he was above the law and would never be held accountable. However, once the facts burst through, Weinstein's lies fell apart. Not only was he fired from his company, but he also is facing charges for criminal sexual assault.

The fact that Trump was a businessman could lead to a truth that he was the "world's most famous businessman," but like many such hyperbolic truths, this truth can't be proven. There aren't any clear measures through which this can be measured, so the truth is easily absorbed by people who want to become successful by learning lessons from the "world's most famous businessman."

The tobacco industry wanted people to believe that cigarettes weren't harmful to them even though the facts derived from research demonstrated otherwise. They largely succeeded until the facts were exposed to the general public, often enough and loudly enough to warrant that warnings be placed on all cigarette packaging indicating the causal link between smoking cigarettes and cancer.

Facts are proven. Truths are believed.

Liars rely on us hearing truths and accepting them as facts. If we challenge their lies as not being true, we get pulled into a never-ending debate. That's because lies promoted as truths are debatable. But if we challenge lies with facts, we make the truths the liars want us to believe less stable and eventually easily destroyable. But if we pierce lies with facts, we can win, even against malignant liars who occupy the highest echelons of power in our lives.

Chapter 2:
Know Your Brain and
Guard Your Fear

Malignant liars have been called many things throughout history—con man, con artist, grifter, swindler, gaslighter, hustler, scammer, trickster, charlatan, etc.—but they all operate in a consistent and predictable way: They lie to get what they want at someone else's expense. These liars use two of our most human instincts against us—our instinct to avoid things we are afraid of and our instinct to trust people who say they want to help us—to get things that they would never be able to get without their loud lies.

These liars are amazingly adept at figuring out our deepest fears, and they use these fears in combination with our default instincts to trust people in order to manipulate us into doing what they want us to do, even if these actions are not in our best interests and even if they are harmful to us.

Given that most of us are reasonably intelligent and have a healthy distaste for liars and lying, it's easy to wonder how malignant liars can be so prolific. How do liars get away with lying as much as they do?

To answer this question, we must start with human biology. As you will see in the discussion that follows, the fear centers in our brains make us extremely vulnerable to believing lies, and that's exactly what malignant liars count on before they start lying to us.

Malignant liars have a profound understanding of their own and everyone else's fears. They know that fear is the easiest emotion to trigger in people, and they know that fear will bring people into their fake worlds, not only as potentially permanent residents but also as ardent advocates of those fake worlds. Fear creates enablers, and enablers empower the liars.

Not all malignant liars fully understand and wield fear as comprehensively as others, but the triggering of fear is a key component of how all malignant liars work when they are manipulating us. The more we understand fear and how it works in the context of getting manipulated by malignant liars, the more we can understand and protect ourselves from triggers utilized by those who tell harmful lies that disrupt our lives.

Our Brains on Fear: The Biological Basis for Why We Fall for Lies

In 1987, Americans were introduced to the now-iconic Public Service Announcement "Fried Egg," in which a man holds an egg and says, "This is your brain." He then points to a frying pan and says, "This is drugs." He proceeds to crack open the egg into the frying pan and he points to the frying egg and says, "This is your brain on drugs."

If we replace "drugs" with "fear," the PSA would be metaphorically accurate as well; when our brains are running on fear, we are reacting with our deepest human instinct: survival. When fear is triggered in our brain, the survival instinct is triggered and takes over our neurology in such a swift and powerful way that it isn't off the mark to compare being under the influence of fear to being under the influence of drugs. According to Martin Samuels, a neurologist at Brigham and Women's Hospital in Boston, the effect of fear is so immediate and intense that, in some cases, people literally can be scared to death.[18]

First, There's Fear

Fear is the most primal and prioritized emotion because, evolutionarily, the afraid survived. If we didn't prioritize fear, we wouldn't be around long enough to experience the other emotions.

Although our fears have become more nuanced and sophisticated over time, our core, primal fears haven't changed much: They remain focused on protecting something that we see as vital to our survival. A quick scan of the most common phobias that haunt our unconscious minds reveals how deeply manifested our primal fears are:

- acrophobia/aerophobia (fear of heights/flying)

- arachnophobia/ophidiophobia (fear of spiders/snakes)

- claustrophobia/agoraphobia (fear of closed spaces/open spaces)

- glossophobia (fear of public speaking)

- monophobia (fear of being alone)

- xenophobia (fear of unknown)

In a way, our phobias are grossly mislabeled: we aren't really afraid of flying or heights; we are afraid of falling to our death from a high distance. We aren't really afraid of spiders and snakes; we are afraid of dying from spider and snake bites. We aren't afraid of spaces; we are afraid of being harmed in a closed or an open space. We aren't really afraid of being alone; we are afraid of not having anyone to connect with (or procreate with). And we aren't really afraid of public speaking; we are afraid of being so terrible at public speaking that we will be shamed forever.

Phobias are triggered by our most primal of fears, and they are fueled by our evolutionary memories. Many people who have these phobias actually have never experienced the harm that is making them so afraid, but phobias don't need us to experience actual harm. They don't need evidence.

We don't need to be hurt by things to be afraid of them. Fear is our deepest and strongest instinct, and if activated, fear will override our abilities to think, reason, and feel anything else.

The Low Road to Survival

For early humans, the world was a dangerous place filled with countless predators, and their survival depended on their abilities to assess and react not just to real threats but also to the possibility of threats. Let's say that two of these early humans are on a quest to find some food when they hear some rustling behind a bush. One of them assumes it's a predator and runs home. The other one takes the calculated risk that it's just the wind or a harmless critter and continues onward to find food. Every time the first person is wrong, they may go hungry, but they survive. The first time that the second person is wrong, they are dead.

The instinct to run is the survival instinct—i.e., the instinct to prevent death and extinction. The curiosity to examine if it really is a predator causing the rustling is the analytical brain overriding its survival instinct to explore the environment in a more intellectual way. It is the emotion of curiosity overriding the emotion of fear. The afraid survived, and the curious didn't live long enough to procreate. And, those quickest to be afraid were more likely to survive than everyone else. We evolved from our quickest-to-be-afraid ancestors. These ancestors were the first to get scared and used their fears to survive. They survived when they prioritized their fears, and they passed along to us this prioritized reliance on fear.

Dr. Joseph E. LeDoux, a leading researcher of our brains on fear—i.e., the brain networks responsible for threat detection and responses—has focused most of his work on the amygdala, an almond-shaped region near the base of the brain that processes and remembers threats and possible responses to those threats. As reported in a 2002 article in *Monitor*, the magazine of the American Psychological Association, LeDoux has found that:

> [T]here are two pathways through which the amygdala's responses to fear can be triggered: a fast "low road" from the thalamus to the amygdala, and a slower "high road" that

passes from the thalamus to the neocortex and only then to the amygdala ... The two paths do not always reach the same conclusions .... The relatively crude "low road" may respond to a long, thin object as a dangerous snake—and trigger an immediate fear response—while the slower "high road" is determining that the object is a harmless stick.[19]

Our primal fears always take the low road.

When the amygdala is triggered, it becomes a dictator in our brain; there is no longer an intellectual, democratic process for managing how our cognitive, emotional, and even physical resources are organized and deployed. When our fear travels the low road to trigger the amygdala, it assumes dictatorship without any conscious thought or permission on our part. When our fear travels the high road, there is a bit more democracy involved: We can reject the dictatorship and choose our course of action even though we are afraid.

Our brains on fear reflect an amygdala dictatorship, a low road triggering our fear responses without conscious thought. When this happens, the conscious parts of our brains become muted, and higher-level functions like reasoning and logic suspended. Our brains on fear don't care to discuss or debate or learn or think; they are focused only on survival. This is true whether the threat is a thief who is brandishing a gun at us, a driver who cuts us off on the highway, a family member who is screaming at us, a bully who is berating us, a boss who is telling us that we will lose our jobs if we complain about something, or politicians who are telling us that our way of life is in danger if we don't vote for them. Until the amygdala relinquishes control, fear will dominate as the primary emotion we feel.

Not only are we not aware when the amygdala takes over our brains, but our brains are hardwired to make it difficult for us to wrest control back from the amygdala once it gains control. If our conscious brains could easily wrestle away control from the amygdala, we would be more likely to make risky decisions—and less likely to survive. Evolutionary ancestors who consistently yielded to the amygdala stayed scared and survived, and we inherited from them an incredible resistance to becoming unafraid of things that we fear.

Fear is the primary portal through which malignant liars lure us into the fake realities they manufacture for their own benefits. Fear also is the anchor that often traps us in these worlds even when real-world facts directly contradict the foundations of these fake worlds.

The Manipulation Cycle: First, Scare Them

The Survival of the Scaredest

"I learned that courage was not the absence of fear, but the triumph over it. The brave man is not he who does not feel afraid, but he who conquers that fear."
—Nelson Mandela

"The Star-Spangled Banner" proudly asserts that America is the "home of the brave." Across the United States and around the world, human beings embrace bravery—i.e., the ability to face and overcome fear—as a positive, even heroic, characteristic in people. People repeat Nelson Mandela's words to inspire courage in the face of great challenges. Sara Bareilles sings that she wants "to see you be brave," in her smash hit song, "Brave."

We celebrate bravery (i.e., fighting against fear) and denigrate cowardice (i.e., letting fear guide our actions). We encourage people to choose bravery over cowardice, but our survival instincts see this human behavior as an existentialist threat. It's the afraid who survive, right? When any of our primal fears are triggered, our survival instincts don't want us to choose bravery. They want us to be scared because scared is safer than brave; scared survives longer than brave.

Our survival instincts cannot allow us to live our lives believing that being brave is always a good thing. So our brains have created a convenient system of neurological activity that allows us to feel good about being brave and still be safe from danger, a sorting process run by the amygdala that organizes fears into conscious fears that we know about and unconscious fears that aren't at all available to our conscious minds. The conscious fears take the high road, and the unconscious fears take the low road.

Conscious fears and unconscious fears trigger the same physiological reactions in our bodies: cold hands, rapid breathing, accelerated heart rate, and increased blood pressure, as well as sweating, dry mouth, and tensing of muscles. The speed of these reactions varies between the high road and the low road. When we experience these reactions because of conscious fears, we are on the high road. We are conscious of the changes in our bodies, and we have time to choose between bravery and cowardice. These are the fears that allow us to say, "I know I'm afraid, and I am good with choosing to not do this" or "I am afraid, but I will do it anyway." We even like to face off with these fears for fun when we undertake activities such as riding rollercoasters, skydiving, and watching horror movies—and the many other ways we like to scare ourselves for pleasure.

But when we experience such physiological reactions because of our unconscious fears, we are traveling the low road, and we have no idea what's happening most of the time. Our response to the threat is determined by the amygdala without any thought or choice on our parts, and the response is to believe, say, and do whatever our amygdala impels us to do to make us safer.

Thanks to the genius of the human brain, each of us can consciously choose to be brave, but all of us unconsciously are cowards who know that the afraid survive.

Better Than Sorry

When do we beat Mexico at the border? They're laughing at us, at our stupidity. And now they are beating us economically. They are not our friend, believe me. But they're killing us economically.

When Mexico sends its people, they're not sending their best. They're not sending you. They're not sending you. They're sending people that have lots of problems, and they're bringing those problems with us. They're bringing drugs. They're bringing crime. They're rapists.[20]

—*Donald J. Trump*
June 2015

Esteban Guzman, an American citizen of Mexican descent, and his mother were landscaping a client's yard in California when a white woman walked up to them and said she hated them. A videotape of the encounter shows the following dialogue:
"Why do you hate us?"
"Because you're Mexicans."
"We are honest people right here!"
"Haha … yeah … rapists and animals."[21]

June 2018

In 2017, I served on a panel discussing the impact of unconscious bias on the 2016 presidential election. The audience of about seventy-five people was a predominantly white and politically diverse audience from a community that hadn't fully recovered from the Great Recession of 2008 and had been hit hard by drug usage and crime. When the conversation turned to implicit biases about immigrants, a woman named Stephanie raised her hand and asked me why it was an implicit bias to not want rapists in this country? I asked her if sexual assault was an issue that was really important to her, and she nodded emphatically and told me that it was a serious issue for her.

I asked the audience members to raise their hands if they had experienced or knew of someone close to them who had experienced sexual assault. About half the people raised their hands. People looked around the room somberly. I acknowledged that sexual assault is, indeed, a very serious issue in many of our communities. I then asked the audience members who had previously raised their hands to raise their hands if either they or someone they were close to had been sexually assaulted by someone of a different race. Not a single hand remained in the air. I paused for a few seconds and then asked the audience to raise their hands if they or anyone they knew had ever been raped by someone who was of Mexican descent. No one raised their hands.

I looked at Stephanie and told her that I agreed with her that sexual assault is a significant issue that we need to deal with in our country but that conflating sexual assault with immigration had led to implicit biases about immigrants, and especially about Mexican immigrants.

I thought I had effectively demonstrated how the facts were counteracting what she was saying, but Stephanie raised her hand again and asked me, "But isn't it better to be safe than sorry and just keep them out of our country?"

Lessons From Little Albert

If I had asked Stephanie if she thought she was afraid of immigrants, she would have said no. That's because most people who are against immigration are angry with or resentful of immigrants, but few admit that they are afraid of them. If I had asked Stephanie if she was afraid of rapists, she would have said yes. Most women have an instinctive and familiar fear of rape and rapists. Did Stephanie realize that her fear of rapists had attached to her fear of immigrants, especially immigrants from Mexico?

Understanding how most malignant liars operate requires us to better understand how our unconscious fears work. Some of our unconscious fears are hardwired through evolution. For example, human beings across various geographies and cultures all demonstrate a strong fear of snakes and spiders even if they have never actually seen a snake or a spider. Scientists have found that "fear of snakes and spiders is innate and has evolutionary origins" because "our ancient ancestors once lived side-by-side with these dangerous creatures" and "those without the innate aversion to hazards such as snakes and spiders likely did not survive long enough to reproduce."[22]

However, most of our unconscious fears are conditioned fears that we develop over the course of our lives, and those that know how to manipulate these fears can condition us without our consent.

Since we prioritize fear as our primary tool for survival, our survival instincts easily can be conditioned to fear neutral or even positive things that are repeatedly presented to us as linked to real fears and aversions in our minds. For example, the first time we ride a Ferris wheel, our unconscious brains may detect the experience (i.e., dangling dozens of feet above the ground in a flimsy container that is swinging in the wind), as a threat to our survival: Our hearts start racing, our blood flows faster, and we may break into a sweat. After the unconscious brain reacts, the conscious brain tunes in and creates a memory that Ferris wheels are dangerous. In reality, plunging to death from towering heights is the actual fear, but our conscious brain translates that into fear of Ferris wheels. Once this connection is set, even seeing a picture of a Ferris wheel can spark the amygdala into thinking we need to protect ourselves from mutilation or even extinction.

Now, imagine that the first time you flew in an airplane you were excited about the trip, or maybe you fell asleep during takeoff. Your unconscious brain did not detect and react to the flight as a threat, so you might not be afraid of flying. Technically, the fear of plunging from towering heights should be greater in an airplane than on a Ferris wheel, but if our unconscious doesn't see it as such, our conscious memories of what we fear will reflect these inconsistencies.

In the early 1920s, behaviorists John Watson and his graduate student Rosalie Rayner conducted an experiment on a nine-month-old child. Watson and Rayner wanted to explore if Ivan Pavlov's conditioning experiments on dogs (the Pavlovian reflex where dogs who heard a bell when they were given food eventually salivated at the sound of a bell even if the sound was not accompanied by food) could be replicated with people. In what would come to be known as the "Little Albert" experiment, Watson and Rayner observed the baby's reaction to a white rat, a rabbit, a monkey, and a few other objects. They noted that baby "Albert" was similarly neutral to all the stimuli.

Watson and Rayner then paired exposure to the rat with a loud noise (hitting a metal pipe with a hammer). Of course, the baby started crying after he heard the loud noise! After multiple pairings of the white rat with the loud noise, Albert would automatically cry when he saw the white rat even if there was no accompanying loud noise. According to Watson and Rayner:

> The instant the rat was shown, the baby began to cry. Almost instantly he turned sharply to the left, fell over on [his] left side, raised himself on all fours and began to crawl away so rapidly

that he was caught with difficulty before reaching the edge of the table.[23]

The white rat initially was a neutral stimulus for the baby. The loud noise was an unconditioned stimulus that caused fear for the baby. After the white rat repeatedly became paired with the loud noise, the white rat became a conditioned stimulus for fear even though "Albert" wasn't scared of the white rat at the start of the experiment. After many of these experimental sessions, Albert not only was increasingly scared of the white rat, but he also generalized his newly conditioned fear of white rats to anything that looked like white rats, such as white furry objects, a fur coat, and even a Santa beard.

If "Albert" retained a fear of white rats as he grew up, he would have a conscious fear of white rats. He would know that when he sees white rats, he gets scared. He would be able to articulate (even if he could not explain why) that he fears white rats, but he might never realize that he cringes at white fur coats or that he just doesn't trust Santa Claus.

While the "Little Albert" study wasn't scientifically perfect, and it would be quite askew of our ethical standards today, it did demonstrate that our brains can be taught to respond in ways that aren't always our original or organic reactions. We can link neutral stimuli to deep fears and then generalize the fear to all things that resemble that stimuli. It is possible to condition our brains to unconsciously respond in this way to all four primary emotions (happy, sad, afraid/surprise, angry/disgusted)[24], but it's easiest to condition what becomes associated with fear because our brain's evolutionary memory remembers that the afraid stay alive even if the fears don't always make sense.

Whether unconscious fears are hardwired or conditioned, they operate in the same way: We anticipate a threat, we mobilize our resources to fight the threat, and we do what we can to be safe. We do this based on what our unconscious brain decides is best for us; the conscious brain is blissfully unaware of how hard our unconscious brain is working to keep us safe, even if we are in no danger at all.

For Stephanie, immigration and the threat of rape had become so unconsciously intertwined that the mention of immigrants triggered in her mind a fear of rape. The feeling of better safe than sorry will guide her thinking on immigration not because of a primal fear against immigrants but because of a primal fear against being sexually assaulted, which in her mind is now unconsciously linked with immigrants.

This shows us how and why the amygdala may stand down after it receives facts, but it never releases the fear that initially triggered it.

This is the key to understanding why malignant lies actually work and how malignant liars can be successful and even rise to powerful leadership positions. They instinctively understand this basic human reaction, and they tell lies that trigger the amygdala. Skilled liars become expert at leveraging this effect and are extremely difficult to counteract.

Tapping Into Our Collective Unconscious Fears

A Black Man With a Raspy Voice

On June 2, 1967, African-American women were wrapping up a peaceful protest at Grove Hill Welfare Office in the Roxbury area in Boston, Massachusetts, when the police inexplicably burst into the building and started dragging out the women. For the next three days, more than ten blocks in Roxbury literally burned as frustrated African Americans, fed up with unequal employment, housing, and educational opportunities, pulled Boston into the wave of urban riots sweeping the country. After negotiations between civil rights leaders and local politicians, the protestors dispersed, and a quiet, albeit tense, calm fell over Roxbury.

Seven years later, in June 1974, a federal judge ruled that Boston public schools needed to be desegregated through busing. In fall 1974, twenty school buses carrying black students from Roxbury to South Boston as part of the busing program were waylaid by hundreds of white demonstrators who threw bricks and rocks against the windows of the buses and hung signs on nearby windows that said "Nigger Go Home" and were illustrated by pictures of monkeys. The boycott by white parents continued for almost two years. After years of mandated busing in the face of white anger and white flight, Boston was deemed in compliance with civil rights laws in 1987.

Charles Stuart and his pregnant wife, Carol, were driving through Roxbury on October 23, 1989, when Stuart called 911 to report that he and his wife had been "shot by a black man with a raspy voice, wearing a black jogging suit with red stripes." Stuart said that the man had "jumped into his car" and "demanded money" before shooting Carol in the head and Stuart in his stomach. Carol died of her injuries later that evening. Doctors delivered the couple's son, Christopher, via caesarean section. The baby died almost three weeks later due to problems related to oxygen deprivation after his mother had been shot. Raymond Flynn, the mayor of Boston at that time, promised to "get the animals responsible" for the shootings.

Boston police got busy with the stop-and-search method, stopping and searching any and all black men within ten miles. The police identified Willie Bennett, a thirty-nine-year old black man, as the prime suspect. Stuart identified Bennett as the shooter from Bennett's mugshot. The police believed Charles Stuart enough to ignore the civil liberties of black men in Boston, and the media believed him enough to cover the crime as a tragedy of the highest order.

In a city sparking with racial tensions, a black man accused of killing a pregnant white woman and her child was as good as convicted. But on January 3, 1990, Matthew Stuart, Charles's brother, admitted that Charles had shot his wife and himself in a premeditated attempt to get rid of his wife, collect the insurance money, and open a restaurant with the money. Charles Stuart confessed his crimes to his lawyer and committed suicide.

Willie Bennett was exonerated, but blacks and whites in Boston were left with the uncomfortable truth that if Matthew Stuart had not spoken up, Willie Bennett would have gone to jail simply because Charles Stuart said that his assailant had been a black man. Charles Stuart was a malignant liar.

Malignant liars know how to tap into our collective unconscious to make their lies feel like truths. Charles Stuart tapped into the racial tensions that had been brewing for decades and rode the unconscious connection that he knew people carried between black men and criminality. This connection is why the police didn't think twice when Stuart said his wife was shot in the head but that he wasn't because he ducked. That is one strong unconscious connection when you believe people can duck from a bullet shot at you from just a few feet away.

What could the police have done differently? Think twice. The Boston police believed Stuart, so they questioned him to get more information; they didn't interrogate him to figure out if he was telling the truth. If they had interrogated him, they would have asked him for details he wouldn't have been able to recall or grilled him on the sequence of events until the facts bubbled to the surface.

Malignant liars don't waste their times with lies that need too much convincing to stick. They understand fear enough to know that if they tap into what a select group of people believe and fear, even the most brazen of lies will have a loud impact. If the people responsible for holding liars accountable in any given context think twice and follow protocols instead of their beliefs, they will find the facts they need instead of narratives rooted in fear.

The Cheering Muslims

On November 21, 2015, Donald J. Trump, one of the Republican candidates for president of the United States said: "Hey, I watched when the World Trade Center came tumbling down. And I watched in Jersey City, New Jersey, where thousands and thousands of people were cheering as that building was coming down. Thousands of people were cheering."[25] On November 22, 2015, Trump was questioned about this comment by George Stephanopoulos on ABC:

> STEPHANOPOULOS: "You know, the police say that didn't happen and all those rumors have been on the Internet for some time. So, did you misspeak yesterday?"
> TRUMP: "It did happen. I saw it."
> STEPHANOPOULOS: "You saw that ... "
> TRUMP: "It was on television. I saw it."
> STEPHANOPOULOS: " ... with your own eyes?"
> TRUMP: "George, it did happen."
> STEPHANOPOULOS: "Police say it didn't happen."

TRUMP: "There were people that were cheering on the other side of New Jersey, where you have large Arab populations. They were cheering as the World Trade Center came down. I know it might be not politically correct for you to talk about it, but there were people cheering as that building came down—as those buildings came down. And that tells you something. It was well covered at the time, George. Now, I know they don't like to talk about it, but it was well covered at the time. There were people over in New Jersey that were watching it, a heavy Arab population, that were cheering as the buildings came down. Not good."

Multiple analyses during and since November 2015 have proven unequivocally that no one in New Jersey—Muslims or otherwise—were cheering on September 11, 2001, when the World Trade Center towers were attacked and destroyed. But Trump's interview with Stephanopoulos shows how Trump taps into the unconscious fear connection between terrorist acts and Muslims, and his added flourish of Muslims cheering allows the connection to vibrate with greater intensity.

Trump knew exactly what he was doing. He knew that the fear of terrorist attacks after September 11, 2001, had soared, and he knew that the fear of terrorist attacks had become linked with a fear of Muslims. By insisting that Muslims had cheered the deaths of Americans in a terrorist attack, Trump fueled the fear of Muslims and created a need for a leader who would make American safe again—from terrorists and from Muslims.

No matter how frequently Stephanopoulos tried to point out that the evidence contradicted Trump's statement, Trump insisted that it happened because Trump knows that the unconscious fears travel the low road while facts and analysis take the high road. By the time our brain hears the facts, the amygdala has already hijacked it and made facts irrelevant.

Trump and Stuart, like other malignant liars, know the secret about how fear works in human brains. People need only imagine a threat in order to get scared. Evidence is not necessary to trigger fear in people, and once the fear is triggered, evidence to the contrary is irrelevant to brains on fear.

The Manipulation Cycle: Then, Sell Them Hope

First, scare them.

Then, sell them hope.

Malignant liars know that their manipulations can go only so far in the real world. Assertions can be fact-checked, arguments can be challenged, and diverse points of view can offer diverse ways of attacking even the most complex of problems. The real world can make manipulation tricky, so malignant liars create fake worlds—alternative realities—where the rules of the real world are suspended and manipulating people becomes unnaturally easy.

Malignant liars are quite creative in weaving these fake worlds into which they want to lure us, but their narratives are predictable and consistent: There is a hero and a villain, and the hero is the only one who can vanquish the villain and save the day.

Master persuaders are rooted in the real world and in facts. Master manipulators, on the other hand, know that the real world won't make it easy for them to get what they want because what they want is to enrich themselves at the expense of other people. In the real world, people protect what's theirs, so a fake world with fake enemies and fake solutions is necessary to get people to willingly allow themselves to be pilfered for someone else's interest.

In these fake worlds that manipulators create, the line between persuasion and manipulation is erased, the lies become the norm, the language of lying becomes the native tongue, and the plot line works to reify the fakeness. Master manipulators know that if they can get enough people into their fake worlds, many people will be afraid to leave or ashamed to leave, or won't know how to leave. If they can get enough people trapped in their fake worlds, they can take what they want with impunity.

Malignant liars know that the most effective lure to use in order to attract people into their fake worlds isn't logic or reason; the best bait is deep-seated fears. The human desire to avoid pain is infinitely greater than our desire to feel pleasure. Our fears are the raw materials through which liars build fake dangers, and once our fears are triggered through the fake dangers, malignant liars know that they can present fake fixes—and fake hope—that we will do anything to attain in order to ward off the fake dangers. Once this fake world has you firmly in its grasp, the malignant liar—i.e., the master manipulator— knows that you will rely on them and them alone to deliver the fix.

The Lottery

Lottery slogans across the United States offer a steady, repetitive drip of hope:

> *Our ticket to dream.*
> *Somebody's gotta win. Might as well be you.*
> *You never know!*
> *Dream Big. Win Big.*
> *Don't let the big one get away.*
> *Today could be the day.*
> *Get our game on!*
> *Winners Happen.*

Millions of people spend their money every single day to buy a chance of accessing hope. The only problem with this promise of hope is that it's a lie. The overwhelming majority of people who play lose, but they keep playing.

What is it about the hope that the lottery promises that keeps people playing even when they are losing their money on a daily basis? To answer this question, we have to better understand exactly how the lottery business works and who plays the lottery in ways that keep the lottery business booming.

Americans spend an average of $70 billion on the lottery every year. That's more than what Americans spend on sporting events ($18 billion), books ($15 billion), video games ($13 billion), and music ($7 billion) combined.[26] Lottery management is a $3.5 billion-industry, and states are reaping upward of $32 billion in tax revenues from ticket sales every year.

States and private companies who manage lotteries rely on millions of people playing the lottery—and playing frequently. But given that the odds of winning the lottery generally are 1 in 175 million, how can you get enough people to play the lottery often enough to generate billions of dollars a year?[27]

States and lottery management companies spend hundreds of millions of dollars every year to advertise the lottery as the premier source of hope for people for whom hope is scarce. Those pushing the lottery as hope are leveraging the fears they know exist in impoverished and demoralized communities: Will I be able to pay the rent next week? Will I be able to afford food for my family? Will I be able to get medical care if I get sick? Will I be okay if I lose my job? Will I find a job that will allow me to take care of myself and my family? Will I be able to move out of a dangerous area? Will I be able to afford to live in an area where my children can attend good schools?

When hope is scarce, fears abound. When fears abound, people are vulnerable to any promises of hope because even just the promise of hope can mute fears long enough to make a day more bearable. Leveraging this human reality, those who make money from the lottery know that promoting the lottery as hope for the people with the least hope—i.e., the people who are most fearful for their lives and futures—will keep people playing the lottery regardless of the odds. As Vox.com reported:

> One in five Americans believes the lottery is the only way they can accumulate a significant amount of savings. This might indicate that people are bad at math, but it's also a sign of desperation. During the Great Recession, more than half the states in the U.S. saw growth in lottery sales. Of the 42 states with lotteries, 25 saw a spike in instant and daily games.[28]

Winning the lottery is a fake dream—i.e., a dream that is almost impossible to attain but is advertised to be the solution to everything if it is attained. People who have the least security and equality in their lives are the most likely to be vulnerable to buying this fake dream. These people often don't have access to chase other dreams—i.e., attainable dreams such as better jobs, higher education, retirement savings, etc. The people who are most likely to play the lottery and spend the largest percentage of their earnings buying lottery tickets are poor people and racial/ethnic minorities who are attracted to the fake dream because it is available to them at their local corner store when real dreams are nowhere in sight.

According to David Just, professor and director of Graduate Studies at the Charles H. Dyson School of Applied Economics and Management at Cornell University, "It's the desperation play ... [P]eople don't treat it like entertainment. Instead those—particularly those who are poor—are treating this more as an investment opportunity. It's their Hail Mary pass to try and make it big."[29] Another study by Just found that although people are generally evenly split on whether they played the lottery for fun or for money, for people who made less than $30,000, 25 percent more respondents cited money rather than fun, while the reverse was true for those with higher incomes.[30] A study by the Consumer Federation of America and The Financial Planning association found that "more than one-fifth of Americans (21 percent)—38 percent of those with incomes below $25,000—think that winning the lottery represents the most practical way for them to accumulate several hundred thousand dollars."[31]

Blacks and Hispanics are more likely to play the lottery more often, pay more for tickets, and spend a larger part of their salaries on lottery tickets than their white counterparts. This is because they see their families and communities as less likely to achieve the American Dream in the same way as white families can. Racial/ethnic minorities in poor neighborhoods have the highest lottery playing rates in our country, leading many economists to refer to the lottery as a tax on the poor.

The cruelest irony is that most states don't even use the lottery money to strengthen their education programs as they advertise. As CNNMoney has reported, "Lottery proceeds don't always get used for their stated purposes. And while about one third of lottery money returns to state budgets, critics say the money tends to replace—rather than supplement—existing funding for the targeted programs."[32] Many states, including Florida, North Carolina, California, and Michigan, have reduced budget allocations for education and use lottery funds to replace previous funds for education. Pennsylvania and

Wisconsin don't use any funds at all for education, and other states roll the funds into general state budgets.[33]

The lottery targets people whose amygdalas are already triggered by their primal survival fears, and they present the lottery as a fake dream, a dream that is ridiculously unattainable but promises to assuage the fearful amygdala if attained.

Instead of advertising it as 1 in 175 million chances to win, they focus on the "every single ticket has the same opportunity to win" message, which soothes the fear felt by people who feel that the odds are stacked against them in their lives and at work.

Those who promote the lottery saturate the culture with the stories of winners and how they can take care of their families and retire well, which offers hope to soothe the fears of not being able to take care of one's family and retire how one wants to retire. The fake dream, over time, becomes less and less about the odds of winning and more and more about the security that comes from winning.

Even a distant hope of security feels better than no hope, so people keep spending their money to buy the hope of getting enough money to survive.

Without the fake dream of lottery, poor people would ask more questions about what society was doing for them to help them get out of poverty, to educate their children, to find better jobs, and to create real hope for a better future. The fake dream gives the frustrations of the poorest among us a place to go, and the lottery industry lies about hope to keep the revenues rolling in.

The fake dream of winning the lottery causes the most vulnerable people to buy lottery tickets, and the money spent by these people doesn't garner security through winnings or come back to them in the form of governmental support. According to the Illinois Lottery, 25 percent of revenues (which translated to $732 million) from lottery ticket sales in 2018 went to "Good Causes," which include public education, infrastructure building, and jobs.[34]

Mario pays into the Illinois Lottery every day. He has yet to benefit from any of their Good Causes.

Mario is an entrepreneur. Armed with torn cloth rags and a charming smile, he rushes to wipe down the cars that emerge from the automatic carwash at a gas station in Chicago. I met Mario when I went into the gas station one day to get an energy drink. He pointed at my energy drink and told me that he didn't need energy drinks because he "ran on hope." Intrigued, I asked him what he meant. He told me that if I bought him a sandwich and a Coke, he would explain.

As he tucked the paper bag with the sandwich, Coke, and chips (because he explained to me that it really doesn't feel like a meal if you don't have chips with a sandwich) under his arm, he reached into his pocket and pulled out several crumpled bills. I watched him smooth and count the money. He had $12. I asked him why he asked me to buy him a meal when he had enough to buy what I had bought him. He told me that "other people can buy me food, but I use my money to buy myself hope." He walked up to the counter and spent $12 on lottery tickets.

Mario is a retired army veteran, and he lives off his military pension, a monthly stipend that allows him to rent a small room in a men's hostel. He has some family in Chicago, but he doesn't see them often. He is afraid that if the rent in the hostel is increased even a little, he will become homeless. He is afraid that if some of his current health issues get any worse, he might die before he gets the help he needs. He is afraid of the violence he sometimes experiences when he tries to wipe down cars.

The only thing that helps him feel better about his fears is playing the lottery.

He estimated that he has spent thousands of dollars playing the lottery over the years, and he admitted that he had won only a few hundred here and there. But, he said, he "knows" that his big win is right around the corner.

Mario's fears are adequately activated by the realities of his life, and his hope in the lottery as his survival tactic is secured. He will continue to "run on hope" despite the fact that the hope never seems to actualize into anything tangible. States and lottery-management companies know this, and they will continue to reap the financial benefits that flow from Mario's hope.

But is the lottery really lying? Isn't this business enterprise doing just what businesses do—i.e., advertise in a way that influences people's decisions? When does advertising cross the line into lying?

John Oliver, host of "Last Week Tonight," explored this in one of his comedic journalism shows and revealed that:

> the massive and massively misleading advertising campaigns for these state lotteries ... those advertisements explain how and why those who play the lottery have come to fall for this con. It's not because they're stupid or innumerate. It's because they've been lied to—repeatedly and constantly, on TV, on the radio, on billboards and buses and from the counters of every convenience store. They've been lied to about the likelihood of winning. And they've been lied to about the purported social benefits of the lottery itself. The state lotteries are sold with lies. And those lies are told with the full authority and credibility of the states themselves.[35]

But there are laws against lying in advertising, aren't there? The Federal Trade Commission's truth-in-advertising laws state that when "consumers see or hear an advertisement on the Internet, radio, in print, on a billboard, on television, or anywhere else, federal law says that the ad must be truthful, not misleading, and, when appropriate, backed by scientific evidence."[36]

And, here is where we realize the malignancy behind the lottery's lies.

Yes, there are truth-in-advertising laws, but state lotteries are exempt from these laws,[37] thus leaving them to lie without accountability regardless of whom they hurt or how much they hurt them.

Liars lurk in many places in our lives. Sometimes they are individuals, and sometimes they are institutions. But they are almost always the party with the greater power in the relationship. The liars are in a position to determine the game, and they set the rules. Once we understand how these games and their rules work, we can be smarter than the lies and play to win.

Game On!

"How dreadful ... to be caught up in a game and have no idea of the rules."
—Caroline Stevermer,
Sorcery & Cecelia: or The Enchanted Chocolate Pot

We are taught about lying and lies in a moral context, so we have internalized the lessons as moral lessons. Thus, when someone lies to us, we feel betrayed and hurt even when these lies occur outside of our private lives. We feel the emotions that we are supposed to feel when morality is involved, but liars aren't playing a moral game: They are playing a pragmatic, amoral game with the aim of getting what they want regardless of what happens to anyone else.

While we are busy shaking our heads and asking how liars could just lie to us, they are harvesting the fruits of their lies. While we reel from what feels like a terrible violation of an important moral code, they are moving on to their next lies.

When liars pull us into their games of lies, we often start playing without knowing the rules. These games don't follow the general rules of social communications, and liars design these games to capitalize on the fact that the rest of us stick to the general rules of social communication.

To win against liars, we must understand the game from the perspective of the liars. Especially in the context of professional and public spaces, a liar's game is not being played on a moral field or right or wrong; it's being played on a competitive field of winning and losing.

To win against liars, we must understand exactly what lies are, which lies matter, and which liars we need to look out for, as well as the neurological reasons behind why we are so vulnerable to believing lies even when we brace ourselves to be skeptical about the world around us.

It is not easy to win against malignant liars without losing your mind, but it is possible, and it begins with the two rules we covered in this chapter.

RULE #1: Recognize that all lies are not the same and that all liars are not the same.

RULE #2: Know your brain and guard your fear.

Now that we better understand how fear works in our brains and how malignant liars use fear to their advantage, we comprehend that these liars are adept at using our fears against us. But, that's only half the story of how fear works. The second half of how fear works shows us how fear works in the minds of the manipulators. Our fears make us vulnerable to their lies, but their fears are what are making them lie.

Section II: Understanding the Opponent

Chapter 3:
The Malignant Liar As
Your Opponent
(Not Your Enemy)

Malignant liars divide the world into people who are on their side (believers, enablers, coattail riders, sycophants) and people who are not on their side (enemies). The liar's use of "enemy" to refer to people who challenge their lies is consistent with the foundations of fear in which liars operate.

An enemy is someone or something which is an existential threat to one's interests: a person or entity that is hostile to one's interests and poses grave danger. An enemy evokes strong emotions in us, usually fear combined with anger. If we play the malignant liar's game, we easily can get stuck in the fear trap of fighting enemies in order to survive. A better way to think about surviving is to consider any liar you want to neutralize as your opponent, not as your enemy.

Fear breeds enemies; games have opponents. The malignant liar is your opponent, another player in a game you must play carefully in order to achieve your goals. To do this, it's crucial to stay focused on your interactions with malignant liars. This allows you to escape the fear center of your brain and access your brain's creative problem-solving areas.

If the two rules of understanding the malignant liar's game are that 1) all lies and all liars aren't the same and 2) you have to know your brain and guard your fear, the three rules of understanding the malignant liar as your opponent are that malignant liars 1) use offense as defense because of their fears, 2) implement a predictable playbook from which they rarely stray, and 3) survive because of their believers, enablers, coattail riders, and sycophants.

Malignant Liars Use Offense As Defense

"The best defense is a good offense."
—Jack Dempsey

Malignant liars are outwardly confident and charming people who manipulate others because they desperately want to be validated, admired, idolized, and given VIP status by everyone they encounter. But their confidence and charm are fragile veneers that hide their real driving force: fear. Malignant liars are intensely afraid that people won't see or treat them in the way they want to be seen and treated if they tell the truth. So, they use their lies as a defensive tactic even though they appear to be part of an offensive attack.

The most common fears undergirding the lies of malignant liars are (in no specific order):

- **Fear of losing**: Malignant liars constantly fear that they are losing (in whatever context they are focused on), and so they will lie, typically using a lot of superlatives, about their talents, accomplishments, or anything else they believe portrays them as winning.

- **Fear of not having or of losing control**: Malignant liars crave control and will lie to gain or maintain control.

- **Fear of not fitting in**: Malignant liars want to fit in and be the center of attention wherever they go. They will lie about whatever they need to so that they are seen not only as fitting in, but as being among the most popular people.

- **Fear of rejection**: Malignant liars are deathly afraid of rejection of any type and will lie to avoid rejection. Many of them consider sympathy to be the opposite of rejection, so they will lie about personal challenges, medical issues, family situations, etc. to seek sympathy if they sense they are in danger of being rejected.

- **Fear of embarrassment**: In connection with their fears of losing, losing control, not fitting in, and being rejected, malignant liars have a stark fear of being embarrassed. This fear is a little different than the other fears in that the liars will lie not just about themselves but about the people in their lives as well because they see their spouses, significant others, children, and other family and friends as potential causes of embarrassment for themselves.

- **Fear of boredom**: Malignant liars crave excitement and fear boredom. Sometimes they lie to entertain themselves and stave off boredom. This fear of boredom also drives malignant liars to constantly seek the attention of others so that they can have audiences for their lies.

- **Fear of anxiety**: Malignant liars are afraid of anxiety, and they will lie to reduce or avoid that feeling.

- **Fear of confrontation or punishment**: Malignant liars do not like confrontation, and they are afraid of punishment. Note, however, that these liars define punishment differently than the rest of us. For malignant liars, fear of punishment is closely tied to fear of embarrassment.

Malignant liars lie incessantly because of their fears. They cover their lies with bigger and bigger lies until something cracks and their fake worlds of lies crumble around them. They game the markets until someone blows the whistle. They abuse and assault until people speak up. They sell fake real estate courses until people sue. They make up stories about black men with raspy voices who attacked them until their own family members confess the truth.

Malignant liars know about the stories about other malignant liars whose worlds have imploded, but one of the core characteristics of malignant liars is that they don't believe they will ever get caught. They have no fear of getting caught because even though they know they are lying, they believe themselves to be smarter and better at lying than the liars who have gotten caught. But they have no understanding of the fact that the ones who got caught also thought they were invincible—until the moment they were vanquished. What's more is that the fears driving malignant liars are stronger than any possible fears of getting caught.

In order to overcome their fears, malignant liars scan the environment to see what kind of lies they can tell that will net them the highest yield of attention, validation, and admiration. They do so with the inherent knowledge of a secret about human beings that most of us don't want to admit: We want to believe them.

Most human beings are followers, not leaders, and we want and seek strong leaders whom we can follow. Although we talk a lot about leadership and how everyone can learn to be leaders (which they can), the truth is that most people have no desire to do what it takes to lead people. For example, only about one third of people in workplaces want to advance into management positions, and only 7 percent want to advance into the highest leadership positions in their organizations. Even fewer want to lead the citizens of the country or the residents of their own locales: Only 2 percent of people in the United States have ever run for office at any level of government.[1]

The majority of human beings are quite content working and living in ways in which they take care of themselves and their families, contribute generally to their communities, and relax the rest of the time. The majority of human beings are followers who don't want to be leaders. Rather, they want a leader they can follow.

Malignant liars see this opportunity and seize it.

Most leaders know how to use weapons of mass influence with dazzling success. That said, some lead through the will of the people for the good of the people while others lead through their own will for their own good.

The former stop where the truth ends; the latter are quick to abandon the truth and rely on lies when it serves their needs for attention, validation, and admiration. Malignant liars reside in this second category.

Malignant liars are everywhere, and not all of them are leaders. But the ones who rise to leadership positions do the most damage to the rest of us. These malignant liars in leadership positions also offer the best insights into the minds of liars like them: We can learn from them and apply the lessons we learn to all the other liars we encounter.

On the Offense: The Malignant Imitation of Persuasion

The first step in understanding the manipulator's mind is to recognize their failure to differentiate persuasion from manipulation. The primary difference between persuasion and manipulation is lies: persuasion uses facts to convince others of the truth while manipulation uses lies to trick people into believing whatever the liar wants them to believe. Malignant liars see no real difference between the two. In fact, they don't actively choose between persuasion and manipulation; they simply default to manipulation because they default to lying.

The difference between persuasion and manipulation begins with intent and ends with truth. Is your intent to create a mutual benefit or a net benefit for another person, or is it to create a net benefit for yourself? Will you be open and truthful about the process, or will you hide information that you know will sway someone toward a different direction? Is there an artistic or a creative intent to inform and/or entertain that is clearly transparent?

Both persuasion and manipulation have a benefit for the persuader/ manipulator, but manipulation is a form of persuasion that uses lies and half-truths to move someone else to believe and/or do something that the manipulator knows doesn't benefit them and could possibly even harm them. "Manipulation can be defined as the exercise of undue influence through mental distortion and emotional exploitation, with the intention to seize power, control, benefits, and/or privileges at the victim's expense."[2]

As social beings, we all engage in strategies to persuade others around us, and that's a natural part of coexisting with other people. But when persuasion resorts to lies, it becomes manipulation. People are most likely to resort to lies when they know the truth isn't enough to persuade people to do what they want them to do. Persuasion is taking the truth as it is and using creative arguments to influence others. Manipulation is making things up and presenting them as true in order to influence others, knowing full well that when others rely on lies to make their decisions, they do so from a perspective that they would not adopt if they had all the facts.

Most us can see this difference. Malignant liars cannot see this difference. They get into leadership positions by charming people, and they stay there by scaring them. While most malignant liars are charismatic individuals, the initial charm of these master manipulators can be explained by three human vulnerabilities that they leverage to their advantage:

- We idolize persuasive leaders.

- We mistake malignant liars for persuasive leaders because they often look alike at first glance.

- We don't understand the full madness of the manipulation that malignant liars will unleash on us.

> *Here's to the crazy ones. The misfits. The rebels. The troublemakers. The round pegs in the square holes. The ones who see things differently. They're not fond of rules.*
>
> *And they have no respect for the status quo. You can quote them, disagree with them, glorify, or vilify them. About the only thing you can't do is ignore them. Because they change things. They push the human race forward. While some may see them as the crazy ones, we see genius. Because the people who are crazy enough to think they can change the world are the ones who do.*
>
> *—Apple Computer, Inc.*

Given the human instinct of fear as a primary driver for our actions, we have to look outside the norm to the unreasonable, the crazy ones, the misfits, the rebels, the troublemakers in order to understand the amazing ways in which we continue to progress and advance in every aspect of our lives. The Apple advertisement refers to the people who hear rustling behind a bush and poke the bush to see if it's a tiger and to the people who see something coiled on the street and get closer to figure out whether it's a snake or a rope. These people are unreasonable and crazy, but they risk themselves—even with the chance of perishing in the process—to help us advance when our collective instincts may lead to retreat.

These people are the leaders that we follow. We entrust them with the awesome gift of prioritizing their directions over those dictated by our conscious and unconscious fears. They use their words, actions, and lives to persuade us to believe, say, and do things that we never thought we would, things that go against every survival instinct we have. We admire them. We respect them. We want to be like them. We are loyal to them. We idolize them.

Leaders who are at core malignant liars are powerful because they can and do override our default instincts through their abilities to manipulate us.

The Apple advertisement has won numerous awards and is frequently used as an inspiration for each of us to strive to be one of the crazy ones. Imagine reading the words below as the faces of Albert Einstein, Bob Dylan, Martin Luther King, Jr., Richard Branson, John Lennon (with Yoko Ono), Buckminster Fuller, Thomas Edison, Muhammad Ali, Ted Turner, Maria Callas, Mohandas Gandhi, Amelia Earhart, Alfred Hitchcock, Martha Graham, Jim Henson (with Kermit the Frog), Frank Lloyd Wright and Pablo Picasso flash in front of you as they did in the original ad.

Powerful and inspiring, right? We idolize persuasive leaders. But, our awe of persuasive leaders blinds us to seeing when persuasion has mutated into manipulation.

Now, imagine reading the same words as you picture the faces of Adolf Hitler, General Mao Zedong, Idi Amin, Joseph Stalin, Vladimir Lenin, Benito Mussolini, Osama Bin Ladin, Kim Jong Un, and Donald J. Trump.

The scary thing is that this advertisement fits this latter group of people as much as it did the former group. When it closes with "Because the people who are crazy enough to think they can change the world are the ones who do," it doesn't specify whether these crazy ones change the world for better or for worse.

We are socialized to follow persuasive leaders, so the leaders who are "not fond of rules" will always attract followers who see the rules as unfair. Leaders who can persuade us to override our instincts utilize the same skills and tools whether they use them for good or evil, but malignant liars don't just persuade us, they manipulate us. They may look alike at first glance, but persuasion relies on the truth while manipulation requires lies. Because malignant liars don't have the same relationship with the truth as the rest of us do, they believe they are master persuaders as they masterfully manipulate their victims.

I have long believed that persuasion required believability, credibility, and truth, but my research on liars has shown me that lies get you as much credibility, believability, and persuasion as truth does, at least in the short term. While truth does prevail as more credible in the long run, if you don't care about being ethically credible, you can just tap into people's fears and offer them a solution to their fears, even if the solution is purely fictional, doesn't solve anything, or will never actually happen.

Not all of us believe every liar's lies, but malignant liars don't need everyone to believe them. They just need enough people to believe them to get what they want.

On the Offense: I Lie, Therefore I Am

If malignant liars came up with a collective slogan, "I lie, therefore I am" would be an accurate one. Lying is as natural for them as telling the truth is for most of us. Recognizing this is the second step in understanding these liars. Manipulators don't know how to get what they want without lying, and they lie because they are scared senseless of what their lives would be like if they had to rely on the truth to be persuasive.

In fact, research studies have revealed something about the malignant liars who use fear to get what they want: They are scared most of all of us. According to psychologists, most malignant liars exhibit to a varying extent a "mental condition in which people have an inflated sense of their own importance, a deep need for excessive attention and admiration, troubled relationships, and a lack of empathy for others. But behind this mask of extreme confidence lies a fragile self-esteem that's vulnerable to the slightest criticism."[3] These manipulators simultaneously need a tremendous amount of attention from other people while they lack empathy for those people. Because of that, they focus on getting attention regardless of what it does to the people from whom they seek it.

If they don't get this attention and acknowledgement of specialness with the truth, they will lie to get it because they are terrified of people seeing the secret feelings of insecurity, shame, humiliation, and vulnerability they are hiding.

In their ultimate quest for attention, malignant liars often seek positions of power to win the adulation they are seeking. Indeed, there is a strong correlation between the amount of fear these liars feel and the amount of power the liars seek.

People who seek power are seeking control over their environment, and they are seeking a channel through which the world around them can meet their needs. Once they find an open channel, they "tell it like it is" using communication tools such as repetition and hyperbole. They also create narratives in which there are villains who must be slayed and claim that they are the heroes who can do the slaying.

On the Offense: Tell It Like It Is (Sort of)

The amygdala serves as the brain's first responders. Not only is the amygdala focused on survival, but it also serves as the gatekeeper for much of what we see and hear daily. When people talk to us, the amygdala processes the information first, and if higher-level thinking is necessary, it patches-in the conscious thought-processing centers of the brain. Our word and speech choices can communicate directly with other people's amygdalas or trigger the activation of higher-level thinking.

Imagine someone running into a movie theater and yelling: "Fire! Get out!" That person just communicated with everyone watching the movie by taking the low road to the amygdala. Before anyone has had an opportunity to fully process what they have heard, everyone is out of their seats and headed to the nearest exits.

Now, imagine someone walking into a movie theater and saying: "We were alerted to some smoke coming from one of the popcorn machines, and upon further examination, we realized that the machine has caught on fire. We think there is a danger that the fire can spread quickly from the concessions area to this theater, and so we recommend that you exit this theater as soon as possible." Within the first few words, each of the movie watchers' amygdalas has handed the processing over to the higher-level thinking parts of the brain because the words don't sound like an emergency even though both scenarios technically are saying the same thing. The movie watchers in this second scenario are taking the high road to the amygdala and will move more slowly to exit the theater.

According to linguistic experts George Lakoff and Jennifer Sclafani, malignant liars' most effective linguistic mechanisms in communicating directly with our unconscious brains are repetition and hyperbole. Repeating words makes them stick in our minds and makes us unconsciously more likely to believe the words are true. Exaggeration is often believed by our unconscious processes even it if is sniffed out by our conscious processes as not honest.

Malignant liars are notorious for using repetition and hyperbole, which often is mistaken for much-needed truth-telling, which ultimately leads many acolytes to claim that the liar is simply telling it like it is. Indeed, "telling it like it is" has become an accepted foil for not following traditional rules of communication. Master manipulators use this to their benefit, even convincing their followers that those who do use a more traditional manner of speaking are fake or phony or inauthentic. In fact, research has found that "sometimes lying can actually make a politician seem more authentic: followers see bald-faced lies by an interloper as symbolic protests against a crooked establishment."[4]

Malignant liars do indeed tell it like it is. We just don't always know what the it is until they get what they want from us.

Malignant Liars Aren't Always Individual Players

We've spent a lot of pages exploring individual malignant liars, but individual people don't have a monopoly on prolific lying. Organizations—formal or informal—can and do create alternative realities to manipulate people into doing things that benefit the organization or people in the organization. Just as organizations can reflect the positive qualities of the leaders who govern them, they also can reflect malignant liars at a systemic level.

If enough individual leaders drive the organization to deliver outcomes based on lies, the organization itself can become a malignant liar. And, as the organization evolves, the prolific lies become part of the organizational history and fabric. The organizations, then, become both fake worlds themselves as well as the master manipulators of fake worlds for their constituents. Furthermore, they operate and attract believers and enablers in the same way as individual malignant liars do: by triggering fears through fake dangers and presenting fake fixes to resolve the dangers. The fake fixes, of course, are ones that benefit the organization at the enabler's expense.

The NRA

The National Rifle Association (NRA) was founded in 1871 to be a firearms education and training organization for military forces and private citizens. The NRA saw itself primarily as a nonpartisan resource for sportsmen, hunters, and target shooters. The organization supported the passage of the National Firearms Act of 1934 and the Gun Control Act of 1968, which were two of the first U.S. gun control laws. It wasn't until 1975 that the NRA got involved in developing relationships with mostly conservative politicians and lobbying for efforts to halt any and all gun control legislation, including bans on semiautomatic weapons, on the basis of protecting Second Amendment rights.

When mass shootings and accidental deaths due to guns started skyrocketing in the 1990s, the NRA came under heavy pressure to support gun control legislation. It had a choice to make: adjust its mission to include reasonable gun control legislation to prevent mass casualties and accidental shootings or maintain its stance that all gun control legislation impinged on citizens' Second Amendment rights. The NRA chose the latter, but the real-world facts did not provide any evidence confirming that legitimate gun owners' rights actually were being infringed in any way, so they had to create a fake world in which citizens were being threatened by violent criminals and all gun legislation was coming from a government that did not care if its citizens had the arms to protect themselves and their families.

"Rob Pincus is a professional trainer, author and consultant. He and his staff at I.C.E. Training Company provide services to military, law enforcement, private security and students interested in self-defense." (I.C.E. Firearms Training website: http://www.icetraining.us/)

On May 21, 2016, during the NRA's annual meeting, Rob Pincus conducted a seminar on "home defense concepts" in which he fervently warned the audience about the danger of armed home invasions and repeatedly stressed that arming themselves with guns was the only way to protect themselves and their families from these dangerous home invasions. He didn't stop there.[5]

Not only did Pincus argue that people should have guns in the home as protection against armed invaders, he recommended that they store these guns in gun safes in their children's rooms for easy access during an invasion because a child's room is the first place you would go during an invasion. He further asserted that if children broke into these safes, the parents had a parenting issue, not a gun safety issue.

On the same day, May 21, 2106, that Rob Pincus told an audience in Kentucky that they should store their guns in their children's rooms, Haley Moore, a five-year-old girl in LaPlace, Louisiana, excitedly anticipated going to see the movie *Angry Birds*. She was playing at home that day when she accidentally shot and killed herself with her father's gun.[6]

During the full month of May 2016, when Pincus was encouraging people to store guns in their children's rooms to protect themselves from violent home invasions, twenty-six children aged eleven years or younger were killed due to gun violence; none of them was killed during an armed home invasion. Indeed, research by *USA Today* and The Associated Press found that a child aged elven years or younger is killed every other day in the United States, with three-year-olds being the most common shooters and victims.[7] This report also found that children are most often killed in the child's home with legally owned guns bought by adults for the protection of their families.

Indeed, protection is the most-cited reason for the purchase of guns. The Pew Research Center's study on guns in America found that 67 percent of gun owners cite protection as a primary reason for owning a gun. Another 38 percent cite hunting, 30 percent cite sport shooting, 13 percent cite gun collecting, and only 8 percent cite their job as a primary reason for owning a gun.[8]

Although protection of self or others is the most-cited reason for purchasing a gun, guns are far more often likely to be used in a crime than in an act of self-defense. In fact, an analysis by the Violence Policy Center has illustrated that for every justifiable homicide (defense of self or defense of others), there are an average of thirty-six criminal homicides every year in the United States.[9]

Despite data such as these, Rob Pincus wants Americans to be so scared of armed home invasions that they buy guns to protect themselves and their families. He wants Americans to store the guns in their children's rooms. But it turns out children don't need to be protected from armed invaders; they need to be protected from the guns in their homes.

The guns are the real threat.

The armed, dangerous home invasions are the fake threats.

On May 21, 2016, in Kentucky, while Rob Pincus was using sleight of mind to spew the fake danger of dangerous home invasions, Haley Moore's life was cut short at age five because of the real danger of guns in Louisiana.

It is critical to understand the fake dangers in the world because they capture our attention and keep us focused on them while the real dangers are wreaking havoc on our bodies, minds, and spirits. But we cannot fight back against the real dangers until we first eliminate the fake dangers. Unfortunately, most of us have never been taught how to identify and neutralize fake dangers, especially the kind created by powerful organizations.

Malignant liars, whether individuals or organizations, create fake dangers using sleight of mind in the same way that magicians create magic using sleight of hand. When you see a magician make a coin disappear, you know that the coin didn't really disappear. You also know that the magician tricked you into thinking it disappeared by distracting you from what he was actually doing. Similarly, people use fake dangers to distract us by making us focus on one thing while they are getting away with something else altogether. And, just like magicians depend on the sleight of hand to make the trick look like magic, the people who create the fake dangers depend on the fake dangers to make manipulation look like power and authority.

With magicians, we know it's a trick, and it's entertaining. With fake dangers, we often don't know when we are being tricked, and it's dangerous.

Rob Pincus is deliberately and passionately connecting home invasions to people's primal fears. Once they are sufficiently afraid, he knows they will look to him for the solution, and he has the solution ready: guns. Guns in our home, guns in our children's rooms. He knows that by the end of his talk, the amygdalas of the participants will have been activated, will have connected home invasions to all their primary threats, and will have accepted guns as the solution. Once this happens, the survival instinct has taken over decision-making processes for the audience members—so much so that statistics about children accidentally killing themselves with guns or increased suicides in homes with guns cannot penetrate the amygdala's tight control on the brain's focus on survival.

Malignant liars' brains (individual or systemic) are dangerous places, but they are remarkably predictable in their *modus operandi*. And, if we can predict the lies, we can neutralize the lies and the liar.

Of course, not everyone falls for every lie, so in the next chapter, we will explore the most likely believers, the enablers, and the amplifiers of lies told by malignant liars.

While it's simple and easy to write-off believers, enablers, and amplifiers as uneducated, uninformed, greedy, deplorable, etc., malignant liars don't just happen upon their believers and enablers. Manipulators select them, and then they manipulate them.

Let's find out exactly how and why they select them.

Chapter 4:
The Malignant Liar's Playbook

Falsehood flies, and truth comes limping after it, so that when men come to be undeceived, it is too late; the jest is over, and the tale hath had its effect: like a man, who hath thought of a good repartee when the discourse is changed, or the company parted; or like a physician, who hath found out an infallible medicine, after the patient is dead.
—Jonathan Swift

Getting away with lying is different from having those lies believed. When most people lie, they lie to be believed so that they can protect whatever it is that they are defending. Malignant liars don't care if anyone believes their lies; they only care that they get away with their lies. Since the malignant liar's objective is to get what she wants at someone else's expense, lies are tools to be wielded at her will, not deceptions that need to be validated by the masses.

Once liars start getting away with lying, they become dependent (or even addicted) to lying and then on getting away with lying. Given the fears (of rejection, of control, of shame, etc.) that drive the malignant liar's lying, the lying can become a source of stability for the liars: It starts to feel safer to lie than tell the truth; it starts to feel more enjoyable to lie than tell the truth. Law enforcement officers and intelligence community members sometimes refer to this enjoyment as "duping delight,"[10] the joy that is derived from getting away with something:

> Initially, they feel joy—perhaps even pride—from lies that succeed. With this comes a smug sense of superiority, which is confirmed each time they dupe a trusting soul. Eventually, they can lie quickly, elaborately, and convincingly. To them, truth (if they still grasp it) matters less than their personal needs. They view lies as tools, and deception becomes a natural reflex.[11]

Most malignant liars are dependent on consistently lying to other people and getting away with those lies. Many of these liars believe their lies will never be aired publicly. Many of them don't care if their lies are aired as long as they were able to extract what they wanted/needed from the situation. "Such liars believe they're immune to discovery, or that they can always cover discovery with another lie. They become the victims of their own lies, but they won't recognize it. Lies are their friends."[12]

Malignant liars don't care if we believe them. Their only concern is that we can't do anything about their lies in time to stop them from getting what they want. For these liars, Jonathan Swift's prediction that "when men come to be undeceived, it is too late" is the goal, so their lies follow a different logic than the average liar's. They practice verbal sleights of hand, distracting us with fake dangers and fake fixes so that we don't notice the plain truth staring right at us. Their strategies can be broken down into four major steps:

1. Use people's trust and truth defaults against them.

2. Twist the truth using an old X+Y=Z play favored by the best of grifters.

3. Baffle people with bullshit using techniques like gaslighting, saying "believe me" followed up with "it's not my fault that you believed me," claims of "just joking," and the amazing verbal trick of knowing something and not knowing it at the same time.

4. Sit back and enjoy as people try to fight back against the bullshit with truth, which not only is ineffective, but also wears people out until they stop fighting back.

Step 1: Use the Trust and Truth Defaults

Malignant liars don't have to work that hard to lie to us because we are born with defaults to trust people and believe that they are telling us the truth—at least until we fully figure out that they are lying. These defaults make sense to our brains because, for the most part, the overwhelming majority of our interactions are based in trust and truth, and it would be incredibly inefficient if we had to verify everything that everyone said to us every single day.[13] Knowing this, we live our lives with what cognitive psychologists call presumptive trust: We approach situations without suspicion that the situation is dangerous because the overwhelming majority of situations we regularly experience are not dangerous. Operating from the defaults of trust and truth is efficient and has a high probability of accuracy, but these defaults also "provide liars with an advantage because people want to believe what they hear, see, or read."[14]

When the amygdala gets triggered via the low road, our conscious brains get muted and we rely on unconscious shortcuts to help us navigate the world around us. Trust and truth defaults are two of these unconscious shortcuts. It takes less cognitive energy to trust someone and believe something to be true than it does to analyze the veracity of something. When our fears are triggered, we want to believe what we hear, see, and read, so much so that we will discredit and discount anything contrary to the first message we receive in order to justify our initial impression, especially if our initial impression was particularly memorable. The more our fears are triggered, the stronger our truth default gets, and the stronger our truth default gets, the easier it is for a con artist to create a fake world for us.

Of course, human beings can be persuaded to override these defaults and act in spite of our deepest fears. However, our trust and truth defaults are so consistent and predictable that con artists have created a simple formula that allows them to use the principles of persuasion with just enough lies to pull us into the fake worlds in which they want us to live: X + Y = Z.

Step 2: X + Y = Z

"A liar only uses the truth when they want their lies to sound truthful."
—Al David

In *The Art of the Con: How to Think Like a Real Hustler and Avoid Being Scammed*, R. Paul Wilson outlines the architecture of constructing a lie that lures people into and traps them in an alternative reality:

> It's remarkably easy to tell a lie when it is accompanied by something real that appears to support that lie ... The process goes something like this:
>
> X + Y = Z
> X = a fact
> Y = a lie (that in some way relates to the fact)
> Z = a desire
>
> I know people want Z.
> They know X is true.
> Y can be used to make Z seem real or attainable.
> Therefore I can feasibly prove the X plus Y equals Z.

In July 2015, Donald Trump was trying to convince the country to take him seriously as a presidential candidate. He knew that for voters, the Z in the equation was having a qualified candidate who had the intelligence and leadership skills to run our country. On July 1, 2015, he said the following in a CNN interview:

> They like to say, "Well, we don't consider him a serious candidate." Why wouldn't I be? I went to the Wharton School of Finance, I was a great student. ... I go out, I make a tremendous fortune. I write a book called *The Art of the Deal*,

the No. 1 selling business book of all time, at least I think, but I'm pretty sure it is.

- Z = People want a serious candidate, and Trump wants them to see him as a serious candidate.

- X = Trump attended Wharton School of Finance and wrote a book, *The Art of the Deal.* These are things that are verifiably true.

- Y = With the Z and X set up, Trump can create a Y: a lie that makes Z more real and attainable.

Trump created Y with a grandiose unknowable item—i.e., "tremendous fortune"—and a verifiable lie—i.e., "No. 1 selling business book of all time." The "tremendous fortune" is grandiose language than can be neither verified nor denied, but hyperbolic language seems much more plausible when someone has written the "No. 1 selling business book of all time." *The Art of the Deal* was then and remains today nowhere near being the bestselling business book of all time.[15]

According to *The New Republic,* an investigation of Trump's claim not only debunked his statement handily, but it revealed that what success the book actually had was a con within a con:

> Contrary to Trump's claims, however, other business books have sold far more copies than *The Art of the Deal.* Total sales figures for Trump's memoir are estimated at between one million and four million copies—compared to at least seven million for *Rich Dad, Poor Dad*; 25 million for *The 7 Habits of Highly Effective People*; and 30 million for *How to Win Friends and Influence People.* And while it's true that *The Art of the Deal* spent 48 weeks on the *Times* best-seller list—even reaching the number-one spot, where it remained for 13 weeks—that achievement was due not just to Trump's image as a celebrity, but also to his vanity and penchant for gaming the system.[16]

The New Republic further reported that;

> The story of how Trump all but assured his book reached the best-seller list was first revealed by Jack O'Donnell, a former Trump executive who detailed his boss's self-dealing in his 1991 tell-all, *Trumped!* According to O'Donnell, who oversaw marketing and served as president and chief operating officer of the Trump Plaza Hotel and Casino from 1987 to 1990, the Trump Organization helped boost *The Art of the Deal* by purchasing tens of thousands of copies on its own. In his book, O'Donnell recounts buying 1,000 copies of *The Art of the Deal* to sell in the Plaza's gift shop—only to be told by fellow executive Steve Hyde that it wasn't nearly enough. "You've got to increase our order," Hyde told him. "Donald will go nuts if you don't order more books." How many more? Four thousand copies, O'Donnell was told.
>
> "We were pressured to buy a lot of books," O'Donnell tells *The New Republic*. So many, in fact, that he had to find creative ways to get rid of them all. "What we would do is use them as a turn-down service in a hotel," O'Donnell laughs. "You know how in a nice hotel they turn our bedcover down and put a mint there? We were putting books on the bed."[17]

Donald Trump had X. He knew X wasn't enough to give people Z (a qualified candidate they could take seriously), so he created a lie, Y, to make Z easier for him to attain.

The fantastic irony in Trump lying about the success of *The Art of the Deal* is that he tells you in the book that he lies as a success strategy:

> I play to people's fantasies. People may not always think big themselves, but they can still get very excited by those who do. That's why a little hyperbole never hurts. People want to believe that something is the biggest and the greatest and the most spectacular. I call it truthful hyperbole. It's an innocent form of exaggeration—and a very effective form of promotion.

Step 3: Baffle Them With Bullshit

If you can't dazzle them with brilliance, baffle them with bullshit.
—W.C. Fields

Once malignant liars know that the trust and truth defaults have been activated, and that the X + Y = Z formula is ready to go, they move on to their favorite step: baffling us with their bullshit.

Before we delve into the tools of bullshit used by malignant liars, let's take a moment to better understand what bullshit actually is. According to philosopher and scholar Harry Gordon Frankfurt:

> It is impossible for someone to lie unless he thinks he knows the truth. Producing bullshit requires no such conviction. A person who lies is thereby responding to the truth, and he is to that extent respectful of it. When an honest man speaks, he says only what he believes to be true; and for the liar, it is correspondingly indispensable that he considers his statements to be false. For the bullshitter, however, all these bets are off: he is neither on the side of the true nor on the side of the false. His eye is not on the facts at all, as the eyes of the honest man and of the liar are, except insofar as they may be pertinent to his interest in getting away with what he says. He does not care whether the things he says describe reality correctly. He just picks them out, or makes them up, to suit his purpose.[18]

In distinguishing between how liars and bullshitters approach lying, Frankfurt is helping us understand the difference between liars who want us to believe what they are saying and liars who just want to get away with lying. Bullshitters say whatever they need to say to suit their purposes, and the following ways of bullshitting are some of the favorite ways in which malignant liars baffle us with their bullshit.

Bullshit Tactic: Gaslighting

Crazy lies are the absolute opposite of truth. Nothing about them is true, but they are told in a way that manipulates us into responding even though there is no truth to them. Crazy lies are bullshit.

Crazy lies are lies that are so obviously not true that the act of trying to prove that the liar is lying can make you seem crazy. Crazy lies are at the heart of the 1938 play *Gas Light* by Patrick Hamilton (later made into the 1944 film *Gaslight* starring Ingrid Bergman and Charles Boyer) in which a husband slowly drives his wife insane by convincing her to not trust what she knows and to believe his lies instead. The play and its many film adaptations gave us the convenient term "gaslighting" to indicate a form of psychological manipulation where crazy lies are used to blur reality and fiction in such a distorted way that makes us feel crazy.

Crazy lies are the fake threats that malignant liars want us to chase so that they can pursue their real schemes without any resistance.

> October 16, 2017 (Presidential Press Conference, Rose Garden)
>
> QUESTION: Why haven't we heard anything from you so far about the soldiers that were killed in Niger?
>
> TRUMP: I've written them personal letters. They've been sent, or they're going out tonight, but they were written during the weekend. I will, at some point during the period of time, call the parents and the families, because I have done that traditionally. I felt very, very badly about that. I always feel badly. It's the toughest—the toughest calls I have to make are the calls where this happens. Soldiers are killed. It's a very difficult thing. Now, it gets to a point where, you know, you make four or five of them in one day—it's a very, very tough day. For me, that's by far the toughest. So the traditional way—if you look at President Obama and other presidents, most of them didn't make calls. A lot of them didn't make calls. I like to call when it's appropriate, when I think I am able to do it. They have made the ultimate sacrifice. So generally I would say that I like to call. I'm going to be calling them. I want a little time to pass.

I'm going to be calling them. I have—as you know, since I've been president, I have. But in addition, I actually wrote letters individually to the soldiers we're talking about, and they're going to be going out either today or tomorrow.[19]

Trump's Gaslighting Crazy Lie: "President Obama and other presidents, most of them didn't make calls."

This lie is so easily disproven that the people tripping over themselves to prove the lie as a lie seem crazy in comparison to the liar. Ben Rhodes, Obama's Foreign Policy Advisor, tweeted: "This is an outrageous and disrespectful lie even by Trump standards." Alyssa Mastromonaco, Obama's deputy chief of staff, demonstrated in her tweet what gaslighting does to rational people: "that's a fucking lie. to say president obama (or past presidents) didn't call the family members of soldiers KIA–he's a deranged animal."

The crazy lies are the hardest to fight back against not because they are difficult to disprove but because they are so easy to disprove that we look maniacal disproving them. But we fall for it every time. We start chasing the fake threat that the gaslighters dangle in front of us, and we ignore the real threat. Perhaps Trump had neither made any phone calls nor written any letters and didn't want us to know, or maybe he was hiding a deeper lie about what actually happened to those soldiers in Niger. Even when we uncover a fake threat, we might not know what the real threat is until it's too late.

Crazy lies are powerful because every time we try to answer a question that never should have been asked, we validate a completely invalid precept.

Keith

Keith was a vice president in Operations in a global manufacturing company. He had just returned to the company's headquarters in the United States from a two-year rotation in Asia and was excited to get reintegrated into the leadership team's structure and activities. He enjoyed reconnecting with former colleagues and meeting new colleagues.

Before a key meeting with the CEO, Jeff, one of the newer vice presidents whom Keith had never met before, asked him to dinner to connect and brainstorm. Keith agreed. Jeff and Keith had an enjoyable dinner. Each got to learn about the other and his ideas for the company's future. During the meeting the next day, Jeff presented many of Keith's ideas as his own in his presentation to the CEO. When Keith interrupted and asked Jeff why he was sharing ideas they had discussed the night before at dinner, Jeff replied by saying that he didn't have dinner with Keith the night before. At Keith's astounded reaction, Jeff asked if Keith could possibly be confused about whom he had dined with because he had been gone for so long.

After Keith sputtered details about how Jeff had asked him to dinner, where they had eaten dinner, and even what they had ordered, the rest of the team looked expectedly at Jeff only to see Jeff shaking his head in confusion. Keith sputtered even more. Jeff continued to shake his head.

Keith gave up after a few minutes.

After the meeting, Keith learned that his colleagues had coined a term for what he had experienced: Jeffstorm. As the CEO explained, "Of course it's a lie, but Jeff has staunch supporters on the Board. So, when Jeff lies like that, we call it a Jeffstorm, not a lie."

Keith's colleagues advised him to protect himself by not sharing unnecessary information with Jeff, getting stuck alone with him, trusting anything he said, or asking him for help in any way.

Crazy lies are crazy not because of the magnitude of their mendacity, but because of the audacity of the gaslighters. In a world where social interactions sometimes require benevolent white lies and rely on people not spewing crazy lies, gaslighters get away with their bald-faced lies because we don't have the tools necessary to call them out and shut them down.

Gaslighting is dangerous because getting people to chase fake threats gives the malignant liar immense power. Malignant liars who are adept at gaslighting can control what we focus on and what we talk about while they execute their schemes uninterrupted. Malignant liars who gaslight are indeed dangerous, but they also are surprisingly consistent with the ways in which they gaslight:

- They tell crazy lies that make you question if they are actually lies because crazy lies seem too easy to disprove to be lies.

- They deny what they said even if you have proof that they said it, and they insist that they said something that they never did.

- They keep the lies coming so that they wear you down, and so you start flagging fewer and fewer lies because you are tired and you know that the confrontation won't result in any changes.

- They will do what they want regardless of what they say they will do, and if the inconsistencies are pointed out, they will deny either what they said or what they did.

- They project their bad behavior by accusing the others of the same behavior without any proof.

- They focus on ways to remind you of your weaknesses and tell you that you are crazy because of your weaknesses.

- They tell you that everyone else also thinks what they think.

Gaslighters tell crazy lies, and they don't care if we know or can prove that they are lying. They only care that they get away with lying long enough to get what they want from us.

Bullshit Tactic: Believe Me

I'm the only one that get the job done ...
Believe me, believe me ...
I'm not tryna find nobody else to beat
I'm the one they come to see because they all
Believe me.
—Lil Wayne & Drake ("Believe Me," 2014)

When do we beat Mexico at the border? They're laughing at us, at our stupidity.
And now they are beating us economically. They are not our friend, believe me.

I would build a great wall, and nobody builds walls better than me, believe me,
and I'll build them very inexpensively, I will build a great, great wall on our
southern border. And I will have Mexico pay for that wall.
Rebuild the country's infrastructure. Nobody can do that like me. Believe me.
It will be done on time, on budget, way below cost, way below what anyone ever
thought. I look at the roads being built all over the country, and I say I can build
those things for one-third.
—Donald J. Trump, Presidential Bid Announcement (2015)

Believe me.

It has been one of Donald Trump's go-to phrases for most of his public life. In 2007, for example, he used the phrase to advertise Trump Steaks for Sharper Image: "Treat yourself to the very, very best life has to offer you. And as a gift, Trump Steaks are the best you can give. One bite, and you'll know exactly what I'm talking about, and believe me: I understand steaks, it's my favorite food."

From selling steaks to selling himself as a candidate for U.S. President, Trump says "believe me" as a direct instruction to our unconscious brain to believe him.

The phrase "believe me" is a signal that someone is lying. Stan B. Walters, The Lie Guy, speaks and trains on interviewing and interrogation techniques:

> Stan Walters listens for telltale phrases that suggest his subject is working overtime to appear credible. When someone emphasizes a statement by saying, "Honestly," "Believe me," "Frankly," "Trust me," "You're not going to believe this," or "Why would I lie?" he's telling you that he doesn't really believe his own words.[20]

Similarly, former FBI agent Joe Navarro warns that "hearing 'believe me' at the end of a sentence or after making a declarative statement always gave me pause. Invariably, I found, there was something more to what was being said if it was followed by 'believe me'."[21] Navarro advises people to "Beware the next time someone utters the words 'believe me.' Ask yourself what they are trying to sell and how important it is to you. If you find yourself being more cautious and dubious, congratulate yourself: You are doing your due diligence."

"Believe me" is a great setup to getting away with lying. By the time we realize that people who can be believed don't need to say, "believe me," it's too late.

Lil Wayne's assertion of "I'm the only one that get the job done ... I'm the one they come to see because they all ... believe me" has a clear artistic intent. It is a piece of music that is packaged and sold as a piece of music.

Trump's assertion of "Nobody can do that like me. Believe me," is a promise to do something for this country, for us the voters, that goes beyond persuasion and is an informal contract that argues that if we vote for Trump, he will do things that help us.

I am a mother of teenagers, an entrepreneur, a writer, a public speaker, and an advocate for many social justice issues. I used to be a trial lawyer, and I used to teach juniors and seniors in college about law and society. I am a consummate peddler and consumer of persuasion, and I do applaud and admire powerful persuaders, but I differentiate between persuading and manipulating. The primary difference: lies.

Trump is a malignant liar, believe me.

And that's no bullshit.

Bullshit Tactic: Lie. Repeat. Lie. Repeat

> *If you repeat a lie often enough, people will believe it.*
> —Attributed to Adolf Hitler and
> Joseph Goebbels

When our brains first hear a statement that is a lie, we accept it to be true because the majority of statements we hear on a daily basis are, in fact, true. So, believing a statement to be true is a rational first response. Eventually, if and when we are given facts that challenge the statement as true, we then assess the facts and determine if the statement is actually true or if it is a lie. As psychologist Daniel Gilbert's research has shown, "[u]nfortunately, while the first step is a natural part of thinking—it happens automatically and effortlessly—the second step can be easily disrupted. It takes work: We must actively choose to accept or reject each statement we hear. In certain circumstances, that verification simply fails to take place."[22] According to Gilbert, "when faced with shortages of time, energy, or conclusive evidence, [our brains] may fail to unaccept the ideas that they involuntarily accept during comprehension."[23]

Lies work because of our truth default, and oft-repeated lies work especially well because our brains need enough time and space between lies to do the difficult conscious work of unaccepting what we accept under our truth defaults. Sometimes referred to as the illusory truth effect, lies that are repeated often are rated as truer by people than true statements because the lies are coming so quickly that we don't have or don't take the time to verify the veracity of the statements.

Oft-repeated lies eventually make the lies sound and feel natural; they feel like truth even if we never verified them as such. Furthermore, the people who seek to disprove the statements—i.e., these repeated lies—don't realize that they actually are repeating the lies as a way to disprove them. That repetition also strengthens the lie, even though these people likely are inadvertently repeating the lies they seek to dispel.

Repeated lies are especially potent when the lies align with beliefs that are already held by the believers. As Politico.com reported:

> Brendan Nyhan, a political scientist at Dartmouth University who studies false beliefs, has found that when false information is specifically political in nature, part of our political identity, it becomes almost impossible to correct lies. When people read an article beginning with George W. Bush's assertion that Iraq may pass weapons to terrorist networks, which later contained the fact that Iraq didn't actually possess any WMDs at the time of the U.S. invasion of Iraq, the initial misperception persisted among Republicans—and, indeed, was frequently strengthened. In the face of a seeming assault on their identity, they didn't

change their minds to conform with the truth: Instead, amazingly, they doubled down on the exact views that were explained to be wrong.[24]

Bullshit Tactic: Not My Fault You Believed Me

The War of the Smartphones has two superpowers, Samsung and Apple, which fight every year on the battlefields of better screens, faster speeds, brighter graphics, more pixels, cooler style, longer battery life, better charges, and everything else you can think of that is connected with their latest phones.

The advertising campaigns on both sides seek to persuade consumers to pick Team Samsung or Team Apple. Both companies have invested millions of dollars to research exactly how to reach potential consumers, and they use color, sound, language, ad placement, and other persuasion tactics to win consumers' attention and money.

This is persuasion at its most dynamic and vibrant. There are competing entities, and each is telling you not only why they are amazing but also why the other entity is terrible. It's a race to see who can be a better persuader, and while some of the tactics may stretch right to the line dividing fact and fiction, the players play fair for the most part.

In 2008, Apple released its iPhone 3G to great fanfare, and it ran a print advertisement that showed the iPhone 3G with the tagline "Twice as fast. Half the price."[25] Within a few weeks, consumers around the world were in an uproar about how slow the phone was and how unreliable its connectivity.

One of those dissatisfied customers was William Gillis from San Diego, California. Gillis purchased the iPhone 3G and immediately became frustrated with the slow speeds and terrible connectivity. He filed a lawsuit against Apple claiming that "Apple and AT&T are disseminating advertising concerning its products and services, which by its very nature is unfair, deceptive, untrue, or misleading within the California Business & Professions Code."[26] Gillis, a seventy-year-old retired executive, accused Apple of lying. Although Apple was able to get most of the other lawsuits on this issue handily dismissed, Gillis and his suit remained stubbornly unwilling to go away.

As Gillis's lawsuit continued to accuse Apple of lying in its ads, evidence mounted that Apple's iPhone 3G ads had crossed the line from persuasive into manipulative: The phone was neither twice as fast as nor half the price of phones that could do what it did. The laws around advertising provide a lot of flexibility for creative persuasion, but they do draw the line at lying.

Apple realized that it could not prove the veracity of its statement, so the lawyers representing the company argued to the effect of "We said something. It wasn't a lie. You thought it was a lie because you thought we were telling the truth. But only a fool would have thought that we were telling the truth. Thus, we aren't lying."

What Apple's lawyers actually said in their legal filing was, "Plaintiff's claims, and those of the purported class, are barred by the fact that the alleged deceptive statements were such that no reasonable person in Plaintiff's position could have reasonably relied on or misunderstood Apple's statements as claims of fact." That's legalese for "it's not our fault you believed us, so what we said can't be a lie."

When manipulators are caught in a lie, they tell you, usually through spokespeople of some sort, that they didn't lie because they never meant to tell you the truth. Get it? Hilarious, isn't it? This little trick is how manipulators continue to lie and continue to don the veneer of persuading when they are really manipulating.

Persuaders and manipulators alike are equally successful at identifying our fears, convincing us to override them, and leading us to do things that we would never do without their influence on us.

Our ability to tell the difference between them before it's too late is the difference between survival and struggle.

Bullshit Tactic: Just Joking

A different version of the "not my fault you believed me" tactic is the "just joking" response. Manipulators use the "not my fault you believed me" to justify lying as a persuasion tool, and they use "just joking" to justify real threats and intimidation to remind you that they can hurt you if you don't do what you are being told to do. These "paper threats" are threats that later are shrugged off as jokes so that the manipulator cannot be held responsible for threatening people to get their way. Ironically, when malignant liars are manipulating you, their paper threats are the only times they are actually telling you the truth, but they have to hide the truth in a joke in order to allow their lies to survive. Let's look at some examples:

July 27, 2016: Donald Trump asks Russia to get Hillary Clinton's emails: "Russia, if you're listening, I hope you're able to find the 30,000 emails that are missing. I think that you will probably be rewarded mightily by our press—let's see if that happens, that'll be nice." **June 26, 2017**: Sean Spicer of Trump's comments: "He was joking at the time. We all know that." **December 2018**: Evidence continues to mount through indictments, guilty pleas, and leaked emails that Trump and his people did seek Russia's assistance with opposition research on Hillary Clinton.

July 24, 2017: Donald Trump threatens Tom Price's job if he doesn't get the votes on repealing Obamacare: "He better get them [the votes]. Oh, he better. Otherwise, I'll say, 'Tom, you're fired'." **July 30, 2017**: Tom Price reacts to Trump's threat by saying on ABC's *This Week*, "Oh, it was a humorous comment that the president made." **September 29, 2017:** Tom Price resigns after a series of scandals following his inability to get the votes to repeal Obamacare.

July 28, 2017: Donald Trump encourages police to rough up prisoners: "When you see these thugs thrown into the back of a paddy wagon. You see them thrown in, rough. I said, 'Please don't be too nice,' Trump said, mentioning observing the prisoner's heads being shielded. I said, 'You can take the hand away'."[27] **July 31, 2017**: White House Press Briefing: Reporter's Question: "The other thing I wanted to ask was, when the President made his speech to police officers on Friday, almost within minutes, statements came from police chiefs across the country criticizing his remarks that seemed to endorse the use of force by police in certain arrests." Sarah Huckabee Sanders's Answer: "I believe he was making a joke at the time."[28]

May 26, 2017: *The New York Times* publishes Jim Comey's notes indicating that Trump asked him to go easy on Mike Flynn: President Trump asked the FBI director, James B. Comey, to shut down the federal investigation into Mr. Trump's former national security adviser, Michael T. Flynn, in an Oval Office meeting in February, according to a memo Mr. Comey wrote shortly after the meeting. "I hope you can let this go," the president told Mr. Comey, according to the memo. **May 27, 2017**: James Comer, a GOP Representative from Kentucky: Rep. James Comer, R-Ky., suggested elsewhere that Trump may have just been kidding. "Comer, a member of the Oversight Committee, says Trump may well have been joking to Comey. 'It looks different on paper,'" *The Washington Post*'s Dave Weigel reported.

Never trust a malignant liar when he is telling you that he's just joking. Pay attention: It might be the only time he actually is telling you the truth. Manipulators often will say they are joking when they hit you with fake threats, and they often will direct other people to tell you that they were just joking.

Bullshit Tactic: Knowing and Not Knowing Something at Same Time

In the real world, if you know something, you can't not know it, but in the fake worlds of malignant liars, you can know something and not know something at the same time. It's a fitting example of baffling with bullshit, and ironically, it works precisely because it makes no sense.

Homewood, Alabama (September 2017)

In September 2017, Roy Moore won the Republican Primary in a special election for Alabama's U.S. Senate seat, and he sat down for an interview with Jeff Stein. The following is an excerpt from that interview (italics added for emphasis):[29]

> **Jeff Stein**: Some right-wing conservatives think Sharia law is a danger to America—do you?

Roy Moore: *There are communities under Sharia law right now in our country. Up in Illinois. Christian communities; I don't know if they may be Muslim communities.* But Sharia law is a little different from American law. It is founded on religious concepts.

Jeff Stein: Which American communities are under Sharia law? When did they fall under Sharia law?

Roy Moore: *Well, there's Sharia law, as I understand it, in Illinois, Indiana—up there. I don't know.*

Jeff Stein: That seems like an amazing claim for a Senate candidate to make.

Roy Moore: Well, let me just put it this way—*if they are, they are; if they're not, they're not. That doesn't matter.* Oklahoma tried passing a law restricting Sharia law, and it failed. Do you know about that?

Jeff Stein: No, I don't.

Roy Moore: Well, it did. The thing about it is it shouldn't have failed because it can be restricted because it's based on religious principles [...] Be careful on the religion [question] because it's very confusing. People don't explain the definition of religion. Put it right at the top, "Religion is the duties you owe to the creator and the manner of discharging it," per the United States Supreme Court, per Joseph Story. When you define religion, we get it all straight. You're free to worship Buddha and Muhammed. The reason that is free is because of Christian principles. Because of the two tables of the law—the first table can't be directed by government. He never gave Caesar the authority over the rights of conscience. In fact, it says it right here if you look right there, that the rights of conscience are beyond the reach of any human power; they are given by God and cannot be encroached on by any human authority without a criminal disobedience of the precepts of natural or revealed religion.[...]

Jeff Stein: I'd like to learn more about the communities in America you think are under Sharia law.

Roy Moore: *I was informed that there were. But if they're not, it doesn't matter.* Sharia law incorporates Muslim law into the law. That's not what we do. We do not punish people according to the Christian precepts of our faith—so there's a difference. *I'll just say: I don't know if there are. I understand that there are some.*

So, according to Roy Moore, there are communities under Sharia law right now in our country, in Illinois and Indiana, Christian communities that he doesn't know if they may be Muslim communities, but if they are, they are, and if they're not, they're not, but that doesn't matter because the anti-Sharia law that Oklahoma passed shouldn't have failed because God never gave Caesar the authority over the rights of conscience, and Moore was informed that there were Sharia communities, but if they're not Sharia communities, it doesn't matter because he doesn't know if they are but he understands that there are some.

Roy Moore knows and doesn't know something that doesn't matter, but he says this is an important aspect of his platform because he wants to do away with the separation between church and state because the separation creates the thing that he knows and doesn't know and that doesn't matter.

If you laughed when you read the above, it's only because you are reading it. Written words have a logical progression to them in terms of how they flow (even the run-on sentences). Our brains cannot follow run-on sentences when the words are delivered in a casual tone with multiple topic switches and nonlinear arguments, so when we hear Stein's interview with Moore, our brains tune out the word salad and focus on hearing only the words that are repeated and on what seems to be the overall message. Listening to this interview would not have made you laugh because your brain wouldn't have focused on the details necessary to find it funny.

Confirmation bias—i.e., the cognitive shortcut to hear what you already believe—also helps our brains sort through verbal word salads. If you are a supporter of Roy Moore, you would have heard that Christian communities need to protect themselves from Sharia law because our government isn't doing enough to protect Christian communities. If you are not a supporter of Roy Moore, you would have heard that he has no idea what he was talking about.

If you started out in the paper world Roy wove with Muslims and Sharia law as the fake threats from which he can protect you if you voted for him, you would have heard what you needed to in order to stay in that world. If you aren't in that paper world, you would have heard what you needed to in order to stay out of that world. But, that doesn't matter to Roy Moore because he wasn't talking to you anyway.

Below is an example of Donald Trump using this same tactic in an interview on *Meet the Press* on February 21, 2016, in relation to his views as to whether America should have gone to war with Iraq [italics added for emphasis]:[30]

Well, what I mean by that is *it almost shouldn't have been done.* And *you know, I really don't even know what I mean*, because that was a long time ago, and *who knows what was in my head.* I think that it wasn't done correctly. *In retrospect, it shouldn't have been done at all.* It was sort of, you know, it was just done. It was just, we dropped bombs. Now if you look back, *actually, that was probably the correct way of doing it, not going in, and not upsetting, giving them a lesson or not.* I mean, I think *Senior actually did a pretty good job of what he was doing.* He went in, he taught them a lesson. What happened is he was taunted. Because Saddam Hussein was saying, "We drove back the Americans. The ugly Americans were driven back, the power of Iraq, the power."

Well, we weren't driven back. He just decided not, General Schwarzkopf and others said maybe let's not go in. *I'm not sure, although I think Schwarzkopf actually maybe wanted to go in.* I think he maybe did the right thing. I can say this, if you look at my conversation with Howard, who's a friend of mine, who's actually a very good person and a good guy, different from what you see on the radio, okay, I will tell you. But if you look at my conversation, I was a very—that was probably the first time—

don't forget I was in business. I was a businessman. I was a real estate man and a businessman. *That was the first time I think that question was ever even asked of me.* That was long before the war took place. That was, you know, many, many months before the war took place. *And you could see by my answer, I wasn't exactly thrilled.*

Baffle them with bullshit, because our brains can't handle it for long enough to engage in a real discussion about what was and wasn't said.

Step 4: Enjoy As Your Opponents Try to Fight Bullshit With Truth

"The amount of energy necessary to refute bullshit is an order of magnitude bigger than to produce it."
—Alberto Brandolini

As *The Washington Post* surmised the day after Trump's announcement speech in reporting on the factual (in)accuracies of his speech: "Businessman Donald Trump is a fact checker's dream … and nightmare. He spouts off so many 'facts,' often twisted or wrong, that it takes a lot of time to hack through the weeds."[31]

When viewed from the X + Y = Z model, Trump triggered people's deepest fears about murder and rape so that avoidance of murder and rape become the Z. X, the fact, is that there is some illegal immigration from Mexico to the United States. Armed with this Z and X, Trump created the Y, a lie, that made Z, the avoidance of murder and rape, more possible. Trump, through linguistic manipulation, created an unconscious (and unsubstantiated) connection between murder and rape and illegal immigration from Mexico. Undocumented people from Mexico became the fake threat that people in this world are fighting, and the wall is the fake dream—the only solution able to be delivered, and only by Trump—that can keep the murderers and rapists at bay.

An undocumented Mexican now triggers the fear of murder and rape in the same way that Little Albert came to fear the fluffy white mouse that he had not been scared of prior to the experiment. Just as Little Albert eventually came to fear anything that looked white and furry, including a Santa beard, Trump's fake threat of an undocumented Mexican immigrant morphs into anything that remotely resembles that, including all Mexican Americans, Mexicans in Mexico, people who look like they could be Mexican, people who speak Spanish, etc. Trump instinctively knows this and stokes the fires frequently enough so that the fake threats seem ever-present and wildly dangerous to anyone inside Trump's paper world.

On June 2, 2016, Trump, in an interview with *The Wall Street Journal*, commented on the federal judge who was presiding over a couple of cases against Trump University. The plaintiffs were alleging fraudulent practices by Trump University that were used to bilk tens of thousands of dollars from unsuspecting students.

U.S. District Court Judge Gonzalo Curiel was born in the United States to parents who had immigrated to the United States from Mexico. Trump claimed that Judge Curiel was biased against Trump and Trump University and had "an absolute conflict" because of his "Mexican heritage." Trump indicated that the "judge's background was relevant because of his campaign stance against illegal immigration and his pledge to seal the southern U.S. border."[32] He went on to say that, "I'm building a wall. It's an inherent conflict of interest."[33]

Given that repetition is key to sustaining paper worlds and fake threats, Trump continued this line of attack on June 5, 2016, on *Face the Nation*:

> He is a member of a club or society, very strongly pro-Mexican, which is all fine. But I say he's got bias. I want to build a wall. I'm going to build a wall. I'm doing very well with the Latinos, with the Hispanics, with the Mexicans, I'm doing very well with them, in my opinion. And we're going to see, you're going to see, because you know what, I'm providing jobs. Nobody else is giving jobs. But just so you understand, this judge has treated

me very unfairly, he's treated me in a hostile manner. And there's something going on.[34]

Trump continued his attacks on Curiel for a few days through various media channels,[35] firmly linking Mexican heritage as dangerous and a wall as the only solution.

Trump's critics went after the infeasibility of building a wall, the racial animus of suggesting that Judge Curiel could not effectively do his job because of his Mexican heritage, and the overall racial bias in Trump's statements. But the criticisms never resonated with Trump supporters. In fact, Trump's critics only made Trump's supporters defend him more adamantly.

While reason, logic, and principles work in the real world, they have no currency in paper worlds. By criticizing the wall and the comments hurled against Judge Curiel, Trump's critics were tricked into attacking the Y, the lie, when Z was really the issue that drew people into Trump's paper house. Attacking the Y only reminds people in the paper house that they are trying to achieve Z, and they dig in to support X + Y because they desperately want to get to Z. The only thing that works to change Z is to go after Z directly.

During the Univision Presidential Debate between Hillary Clinton and Donald Trump in March 2016, Clinton mocked Trump's wall:

> First of all, as I understand him, he's talking about a very tall wall, a beautiful tall wall, the most beautiful tall wall, better than the Great Wall of China, that would run the entire border. He would somehow magically get the Mexican government to pay for it. It's just fantasy.[36]

She responded to Trump's paper-world bullshit with real-world facts. It did not work. Clinton attacked the Y in the equation without addressing the Z, the foremost issue on people's minds. If she had recognized the con, she could have dismantled the con. An ideal response from her would have been something like:

- "I know how important it is to secure our borders. The President's job is to secure the safety of every man, woman, and child in our country, and we should explore all opportunities to keep our borders safe." (The Z is being addressed directly here.)

- "Building a wall is one way to secure our borders, but there are other ways that will work better and better ensure our safety. Our safety comes first. Always." (Z is being addressed again, and the response agrees that Trump's Y is a possibility, but it dismisses it as not the best option. This makes the lies not worth arguing about. The response reiterates that safety is first.)

The above response neutralizes the con game by identifying and validating Z and minimizing Y.

Chapter 5:
The Malignant Liar's Team:
Believers, Enablers, and
Coattail Riders

Malignant liars cannot win on their own. These liars rely on three different and often overlapping groups of people to maintain their lies: believers, enablers, and coattail riders.

Believers believe the lies: They are lured into the fake worlds, and they wholeheartedly believe the fake dangers and the fake fixes. Believers believe that if these fake dangers are slayed with the fake fixes, their lives will change for the better, and they are cheering for the liar to be successful as a proxy for their own survival and success.

Enablers don't always believe the lies, but they help the manipulators maintain the lies. Even though they don't believe the lies, they do believe their lives will be better off with these liars in charge in relation to the alternatives. Enablers would never be brazen enough to lie as prolifically as the malignant liars they choose to believe, but they will twist the truth and venture into the land of lies to make sure that the liars they are supporting don't go down in flames.

Coattail riders are happy to tag along on the manipulator's coattails and take a slice of the ill-gotten pie for themselves. They also strive to keep their hands clean by supporting the liar in indirect ways that don't require them to confront the lies being told or tell any lies themselves.

Believers take up residence in the fake worlds created by the liars; enablers make sure that the fake world stays intact for the believers; and coattail riders support the fake worlds from a distance so that they benefit from the lies without having to wade in the lies themselves.

Malignant liars understand these groups well, and they strategically nurture them even if some of the strategy is just learned behavior from their lifetimes of lying. These liars can quickly identify who goes into which group, and if they cannot fit you into one of these three groups, you become their opponent, and in more hyperbolic cases, their enemy.

The Believers

*You cannot reason people out of a position that they did not
reason themselves into.*
—Ben Goldacre

Malignant liars are excellent at identifying and creating believers. In addition to taking advantage of people's trust and truth defaults, these liars instinctively know what experts in lying and lie detection have proven repeatedly: "Humans aren't very good at being able to tell—just from watching someone and listening to them talk—whether they are being told truth or fiction."[37] What we believe to be true is shaped by what we already believe to be true, an outgrowth of the confirmation bias at work in our brains.

For example, about 20 percent of Americans believe that vaccinations cause autism even though dozens of studies have disproven the link. As one researcher explains:

> We vaccinate most children, so most autistic children will have been vaccinated. This doesn't show that vaccinations cause autism. All vaccinated children will want to stay up late, but no one thinks vaccinations cause that! Moreover, many huge studies have unequivocally shown that vaccinations don't cause autism. Why do people still believe vaccinations cause autism? Because it was their existing belief and no other explanation for autism has displaced it. In this context, the fact that all kids with autism have been vaccinated seems compelling supporting evidence.[38]

If someone believes that vaccinations cause autism, information about vaccinations causing autism "feels" true, and the overwhelming amount of information showing that vaccinations don't cause autism "feels" false. We are more likely to attribute honesty to information that "feels" true and lying to information that "feels" false.

An important aspect of confirmation bias is that when people believe or disbelieve someone or something based on confirmation bias, information to the contrary is not accepted by the brain. Thus, the biased belief remains immune to information that disproves the belief.

Selling the Eiffel Tower ... Twice

Parisians were not happy with the rusting metal tower that had been built in 1889 for the Paris Exposition and was never torn down as intended. Expensive to maintain and declining in popularity, the Eiffel Tower was not a pleasant topic of conversation for anyone in Paris in 1925.

But Victor Lustig didn't see an ugly metal tower when he saw the Eiffel Tower; instead, he saw an opportunity.

Lustig researched scrap metal dealers in Paris and invited (on beautifully forged government stationery) the six largest dealers to a private meeting at one of the most esteemed Parisian hotels, the Hôtel de Crillon, to discuss a confidential business deal. All six dealers came to the meeting. After introducing himself as the Deputy Director-General of the Ministry of the Posts, Lustig congratulated the dealers on being selected for the business opportunity because of their reputations as good and honest businessmen. Lustig then solemnly told the dealers that Paris could no longer keep up with the maintenance and repair costs of the aging Eiffel Tower. He added that the city was quietly seeking to sell it simply for the scrap value of the thousands of pounds of metal.

The six men were taken in a private limousine to tour the Eiffel Tower and asked for their discretion in keeping the matter quiet as they developed their bids for the deal, which Lustig told them were due the very next day.

While the dealers were sizing up their competition and the value of the business deal, Lustig was sizing up the dealers to see which of them he wanted to select for his plan. He picked André Poisson, the poorest, most insecure, and least connected of the dealers. He could tell Poisson was the most afraid of not being accepted by the other dealers, and that he was the most desperate to get the deal. Lustig played on Poisson's fears and told Poisson that he had been selected but Lustig wasn't sure if he could really sell to him. Lustig demanded an elevated level of secrecy around the negotiations and payment logistics.

Poisson was excited to be selected but grew suspicious at the increasing secrecy of the dealings. Expecting this, Lustig "confessed" to Poisson that he knew how underhanded he must appear and shared with Poisson that he was being secretive because he was hoping for an under-the-table payment from Poisson to make the deal go through without a hitch. He traded on Poisson's default instinct to trust by telling him that he was really on Poisson's side but needed some extra money.

Poisson was relieved at the request for a bribe because that was exactly the type of behavior he expected from a Parisian bureaucrat (confirmation bias), and hearing Lustig's "confession" eased Poisson's fears. Poisson paid Lustig a total of $70,000, which included the deposit on the bid as well as the bribe.[39]

When Poisson finally realized that the Eiffel Tower was not for sale, he never filed a complaint because he was too embarrassed to tell people that he had been taken for a fool. The same things that made Poisson vulnerable to Lustig's lies kept him from reporting the conman.

Victor Lustig was a malignant liar who created a fake reality in which the Eiffel Tower was for sale. He targeted a victim whose fears and desires would make him most vulnerable to Lustig's lies. Lustig got what he wanted—at Poisson's expense—but victories like this don't satisfy malignant liars; they only whet their appetites to do it again. Indeed, Lustig ran the Eiffel Tower scheme again just months later. This time, however, the winning bidder did report him. Lustig went down in history as the "man who sold the Eiffel Tower … twice."

When Victor Lustig invited the Parisian metal dealers to the Hôtel de Crillon, he was creating a fake world that had its own rules and logic. Poisson and the others didn't know they were entering this fake world with its own rules of logic. Indeed, the madness of manipulation lies in the fact that the manipulators are creating these rules and logic to benefit themselves; when we enter these fake worlds, we don't know that we are leaving the real world behind. In this fake world, not only did Lustig's secrecy make logical sense to the dealers, but asking for a bribe to keep the secret made even more sense.

Believers and Rational Irrationality

People almost invariably arrive at their beliefs not on the basis of proof but on the basis of what they find attractive.
—Blaise Pascal

Malignant liars lure their believers into fake worlds where they can manipulate them into doing what they want. Once believers have entered these worlds, some choose to stay even in the face of growing evidence that the fake world isn't real. These believers are people who are convinced that they cannot achieve what they want without the malignant liar's help. In a rationally irrational way, they find it more beneficial to believe the lies than to confront the truth.

Not only do they not want to confront the truth, but many believers even refuse to believe the truth when they hear it. The perceived safety of the fake world in which they believe they have control, illusory as it may be, feels better than the real world, where their lack of control is all too real. Believe it or not, this is not irrational: It's rationally irrational.

None of us likes being called irrational. As a matter of fact, our primary responses to being called irrational are emotional and quite irrational. Our intellect understands the word irrational as something not being rooted in reason, logic, evidence, or even just common sense. Our emotions, however, understand irrationality quite differently. Our emotional understanding of the word is that when someone is irrational, that person isn't making sense because they are disagreeing with us. In other words, if someone disagrees with us, and they refuse to be persuaded by us, well, rationally speaking, they are therefore irrational! Emotionally speaking, when people understand and agree with our reasoning, they are rational (and make us feel good); when they don't understand and agree with our reasoning, they are irrational (and make us feel bad).

We have maligned the word irrational so much that we have created a new term—rational irrationality—to help us redefine and accept the irrationality that influences more of our behaviors than we would like to admit. We become upset when someone calls us irrational, but most of us can live with being called rationally irrational.

Rational irrationality is a paradox, but it is a paradox that allows us to understand our emotions (without our emotions getting in the way). It does so by decoupling irrationality from its negative connotations of being unhinged or unreasonable. Rational irrationality allows us to analyze the choices we make that are rooted in emotion, as opposed to reason or logic, without denigrating those choices as automatically negative.

Let's say that you need to get from Point A to Point B in thirty-five minutes, and the distance between the two is twenty miles. A direct road between A and B will let you make the trip in about twenty. A circuitous road from A to B will take you about forty-five minutes. The most rational choice is for you to take the direct road because the circuitous road will get you there ten minutes late, and the lateness will be an embarrassment for you and your family.

You are about to take that direct route when your best friend tells you that the direct road between A and B goes through a dangerous neighborhood and that you should be careful driving with your family through that neighborhood. Your first instinct is to ask how dangerous the neighborhood really is and whether it is dangerous enough to warrant more than doubling the amount of time to make the trip. Your best friend tells you that even though they have never heard of anything happening to anyone, they have heard that it's a "really bad neighborhood" and "not worth the risk." You trust your best friend, and you can hear how seriously they are warning you. You decide that being ten minutes late is better than taking a ride through a dangerous neighborhood and that it's better to be safe than sorry.

The direct route is the most rational choice. If the direct route had been closed, leaving the circuitous route as the only option, the circuitous route would be the most rational choice. Taking the circuitous route and being late when a direct route that gets you there on time is available is an irrational choice; however, if you believe (without any evidence) that the direct route is somehow not in your best interest, the circuitous route becomes a rationally irrational choice.

Rational irrationality refers to the nonrational decisions that people make when 1) certain beliefs are more important to people than evidence or truth, and 2) the cost of doing the irrational thing is relatively low. In the hypothetical above, the fear of danger and the trust in your best friend creates a belief of risk that is more important in that moment than researching the crime rates in that particular neighborhood to make a rational decision. More important, even if you did do that research and you found no evidence that it was any more dangerous than any neighborhood that you would go through on the circuitous route, the belief that it's better to be safe than sorry will cause you to downgrade the value of the research in relation to your friend's warning because your friend's warning is the more risk-averse choice.

You also are more likely to choose the circuitous route when the cost of doing so is relatively low. If you are going to be ten minutes late, and that's not too big of a deal, it becomes easier to take the nonrational route. But, let's say that this isn't a leisurely family trip. Let's say that it's the job interview that you have been anticipating for weeks. Let's further stipulate that that ten-minute tardiness will kick you out of the running. When the cost of doing the irrational thing increases, your brain will have a more difficult time justifying the nonrational choice and nudge you to choose the rational choice.

When your beliefs about something are strong, and your costs of acting on that belief in lack of or even contrary to the evidence are low, you are highly likely to be rationally irrational. When you are rationally irrational, you relax your analytical and reasoning frameworks, ignore facts and evidence, and rely on cognitive biases and emotional appeals. According to Michael Huemer, professor of philosophy at University of Colorado–Boulder, the following are a few of the primary contexts when beliefs override rationality:

- **Consistency and Coherence**: people adopt and hold beliefs that are consistent and coherent with their existing beliefs.

- **Social Bonding**: people adopt and hold the same beliefs as people whom they like and want to associate with in order to belong to a social community.

- **Self-Image**: people hold beliefs that fit with the self-image they want to adopt and/or project for reasons of group status and group acceptance—e.g., if someone wants to be seen as religious, even if he is not religious, he might hold beliefs that he perceives religious people as holding.

- **Self-Interest**: people hold beliefs that benefit themselves and/or the groups with whom they identify (e.g. racial/ethnic group, family group, religious group, community group, regional/local geographic group, work/career group, etc.); self-interest sometimes also can include identification with groups that people don't belong to but want to belong to (e.g. celebrities, athletic teams, etc.); and it can include boosting self-interest through denigration of other groups.

When these contexts are present, people will more often than not miss or misinterpret information that they are receiving if it challenges or contradicts their beliefs. It's easy to observe this from outside people's lives and wonder if they are being delusional or acting against their own interests. But the pull to be rationally irrational is about people prioritizing what's most important to them. We all make rationally irrational decisions in our lives, and while those outside our lives focus on the irrationality of our choices, we rest assured in the rationality of making that irrational choice.

All of us are vulnerable to lies that malignant liars tell, but the truth is that there are some things that make some people more vulnerable than others to becoming believers for manipulators. The differentiated vulnerabilities to lies can help us forecast who is more likely to get lured into the fake worlds that malignant liars weave, and it can help us understand and be more empathetic to why believers believe and do what they do.

Recall that when our fears are triggered, our amygdalas hijack full control of our brains until the fear is resolved and made irrelevant in other ways. When malignant liars trigger our fears via the low road, we go into amygdala-controlled mode without conscious intent or permission. The truth about believing lies is that some of our amygdalas are more prone to getting hijacked than others, making some of us more vulnerable to alternate realities, fake worlds, fake threats, and fake fixes.

Rational Irrationality: Consistency

None of us sees (or wants to see) ourselves as insecure, powerless creatures that have no control over our lives. So, if we find ourselves in situations where we feel this way, we become vulnerable to being easy prey for malignant liars.

All of us can be rationally irrational at times, but a lack of control—i.e., feeling insecure about something—can make us especially susceptible to rationalizing our belief in something even when there is evidence to the contrary. Our brains can literally make up things (self-deception) or make up contexts in which someone else's lies can, ostensibly, be the truth. The less control you feel about areas in your life that are important to you, the more likely you are to see "facts" that don't exist anywhere other than in your mind in order for you to live in a reality that is consistent with what you want to be true about yourself.

Jennifer Whitson, an Assistant Professor of Management and Organizations at UCLA, and Adam Galinsky, Chair of Management Division at Columbia University, have studied the effects of insecurity on people's tendency to believe lies. They found that the more insecure or vulnerable someone feels, the more likely that person is to believe lies. The bigger the lie, the more insecure someone has to feel to believe it. As Galinsky explains:

> The less control people have over their lives, the more likely they are to try and regain control through mental gymnastics. Feelings of control are so important to people that a lack of control is inherently threatening. While some misperceptions can be bad or lead one astray, they're extremely common and most likely satisfy a deep and enduring psychological need.[40]

Our need to feel in control helps us stave off fear, and that need overrides everything else, even facts.

The Rattlesnake King

Rheumatism was first described by Augustin Jacob Landré-Beauvais, a twenty-eight-year-old physician at the Saltpêtrière asylum in France in 1800. "Unlike gout, this condition [rheumatism] mainly affected the poor, affected women more often than men, and had previously been ignored by other physicians who—concerned with earning acclaim and compensation for their work—usually chose to treat more affluent patients."[41]

The 1800s ushered in a relatively terrible time of healthcare for American people. There were very few doctors, and those who were around were eschewing science (as were their European counterparts) and utilizing medical protocols such as bleeding and purging. "The public envisioned poverty as the cause of disease and not disease the result of poverty and poor living conditions. Political leaders believed that low morals predisposed people to bad health; thus, the poor were responsible for their own sicknesses."

With maladies like rheumatism relegated to being suffered by those who weren't wealthy, most people in the 1800s felt hopeless about their pain and insecure and afraid about their futures because pain from things like rheumatism kept them from being able to work and provide for their families.

Given the persistent belief that good men and women—especially those in the middle and working classes—are supposed to work hard and provide for their families, the inability to take care of health issues becomes inconsistent with what good men and women should do. As discussed, when reality is inconsistent with your beliefs, you relax your analytical and reasoning frameworks, ignore facts and evidence, and rely on cognitive biases and emotional appeals so that reality (even if it's a manufactured one) is consistent with your beliefs.

It's no wonder that this environment was ripe for a snake oil salesman with fake remedies and false hopes to swoop in and take advantage of people's insecurities and fears about their health, general welfare, and future and give them an alternative reality that was consistent with who they believed they were.

In 1893, the World Columbian Exposition in Chicago drew more than 27 million visitors (roughly 25 percent of the United States population at the time) to a dazzling display of architecture and innovation. In crowded spaces where more than sixty-five thousand innovations were displayed and marketed, Clark Stanley stood out as someone who knew how to get and keep people's attention. Dressed in an eclectic and colorful outfit borrowed from cowboy fashions and Native American prints, Stanley enraptured crowds with his dramatic tale of traveling to Walpi, Arizona, and learning mystical medicinal secrets from a Hopi medicine man.

As Stanley told the crowd about how he learned about the medicinal miracle of snake oil from his Hopi teacher, he pulled out a rattlesnake from a bag, beheaded it, sliced it down the middle, and threw it into a pot of boiling water. He waited for the crowd to catch their breaths and then showed them how fat was rising to the top of the boiling water. He scooped up the fat, bottled it, and sold it on the spot as an amazing and guaranteed cure for rheumatism, pains, aches, sprains, bruises, frostbite, insect bite, lame back, and myriad other ailments. It was Clark Stanley's Snake Oil Liniment.

For decades, Stanley traveled the country, killing rattlesnakes in front of crowds. He sold his Clark Stanley's Snake Oil Liniment so successfully that he opened several manufacturing facilities and could barely keep up with the demand for his miraculous snake oil.

Stanley then wrote a book in 1897 titled *The Life and Adventures of the American Cowboy*, with the author's name written as "Clark Stanley, Better Known As the Rattle Snake King" to market his brand and entice more customers to trust the snake oil from a cowboy who learned medicine from the Hopi.

Clark Stanley used the gleam of the World's Columbian Exposition to portray success, and he used the authority lent by his book to keep the momentum going. The proprietary formula of his magical liniment, with its mystical Hopi roots, and the sensational rattlesnake slayings indicated that he alone had something unique and not available elsewhere. Only he could guarantee the success of his potion. Together, all of this alleviated any feelings of caution or risk among his potential customers.

In 1906, the United States passed the Pure Food and Drug Act to ensure accuracy of ingredients in food and drug products. In 1910, scientists tested Clark Stanley's Snake Oil Liniment under the Pure Food and Drug Act and found no snake oil in the product. Instead, they found that the liniment contained mineral oil, red pepper, camphor, turpentine, and a touch of fatty oil. Stanley paid a small fine, but he became the original snake oil salesman, the term used to describe anyone selling a jar of lies.

Unlike armed criminals who take what they want through the threat of injury or death, snake oil salesmen promise us something good, take our money, and give us something that is no good. But they are able to maintain the con so that we believe we have something good and are much happier with our experiences in this alternative reality than we are with realities in the real world.

Stanley's fake reality was a world in which the fake fix of the snake oil was the only thing that could cure the illnesses that debilitated the lives of people who were not wealthy. Without the snake oil, there was suffering. With the snake oil, there was health.

Once a fake reality is created, we can't get enough of the fake solution, no matter how much chasing that fix costs us because the fake reality is more consistent with what we want to believe about ourselves than anything we could find in the real world. We become invested in maintaining the fake world and touting the benefits of the fake fix because we don't want to go back to a world where we suffered without being able to do anything about it. The sense of control (albeit fake) we find in the alternative reality is better than the lack of control we experience in the real world.

Stanley created a world for his believers, and his believers sustained that world for Stanley.

Rational Irrationality: Social Bonding

> *"Lies sound like facts to those who've been conditioned to*
> *mis-recognize the truth."*
> —DaShanne Stokes

Social bonds are critical to our survival. They keep us connected, healthy, and happy. However, there is an underbelly to social bonds that makes us vulnerable to malignant liars: groupthink. Groupthink happens when a people in a group have a strong shared identity and feel conscious or unconscious pressure to conform to a particular ideal or take a particular course of action. Even for the most rational and analytical people, group social bonds can serve as verification processes that obscure data gaps or logic errors that they likely otherwise would notice.

When malignant liars tap into groupthink, they can effectively and efficiently create believers. Lies become easy to maintain because tough questions are not being asked, and the alternative reality becomes a self-sustaining entity as believers validate the process without necessarily realizing it. Sometimes, especially in the case of financial frauds, these realities crumble from a lack of sustainability and resources. But they only do so after wreaking mass destruction in many lives and communities.

The Madoff Madness

Bernard Lawrence "Bernie" Madoff, former nonexecutive chairman of the NASDAQ and founder of Bernard L. Madoff Investment Securities LLC, financially defrauded his clients in the largest Ponzi scheme in American history to the tune of approximately $65 billion. He pled guilty to eleven felonies and was sentenced to one hundred fifty years in prison. Although Stanley, the Rattlesnake King, defrauded everyday Americans who may or may not have had the resources to double-check their truth default, Bernie Madoff defrauded the likes of Steven Spielberg, Kevin Bacon, Elie Weisel, Jeffrey Katzenberg, and Larry King, wealthy, successful people who had access to resources and experts, all of which could have helped them detect and avoid a fraud of this magnitude.

Unfortunately, resources and experts are no match for a good malignant liar. Madoff targeted wealthy Jewish people because he knew that playing on their common heritage would add a layer of trust that intensified the truth default. He knew that they would want to believe him, and so they would. Madoff then applied classic snake-oil salesman tactics to building his fraudulent business: visible and even flashy success (e.g., office in downtown Manhattan, membership in all the right clubs, invitations to the right events, etc.), proprietary "magic" formula (e.g., split-strike strategy), and guaranteed success (e.g., no losses—ever).

Both Stanley and Madoff made a lot of money as malignant liars, and neither ever expressed true remorse about the lies they told or for the people who believed the lies to their detriment. How do malignant liars feel about the people they lie to? In jail, when Madoff's lies could no longer garner any value for him, he voiced his true feelings about those he had lied to: "Fuck my victims."[42]

Rational Irrationality: Self-Image

The concept of self-image is best understood through the dynamic lens of status:

"where we are positioned in relation to those around us: literally where we are in the "pecking order." Your perception of status, and any changes in it, can be a driver of what's called primary reward or threat. A sense of increasing status can be more rewarding than money, and a sense of decreasing status can feel like your life is in danger.[43]

Although we have adopted Darwin's "survival of the fittest" and "natural selection" concepts into everyday parlance, the evolutionary psychology that governs our emotions is equally salient in our interactions today.

For our ancient ancestors (and especially for men), status in tribal groups was related to demonstration of physical strength, robust health, and virility, all of which connoted the ability to reproduce strong and healthy children. In those times and now, societies created games, rituals, and battles with clear winners and losers (losing often meant death!) for males to demonstrate their winner status. Males who emerged as winners were seen as powerful leaders. By virtue of this status, those who were like the winners and who existed within the winners' inner circles enjoyed a higher status by proxy.

Malignant liars understand this dynamic in a deeply instinctive way, and they use the language of winning to position themselves as powerful leaders and to attract believers who want to win by proxy. For many, that ancient instinct to cow to the winner triggers enabling behavior when manipulators start talking about winning, even when manipulators are lying.

The language of winning is a direct route to rational irrationality.

Sick and Tired of Winning

"We're going to win. We're going to win so much. We're going to win at trade, we're going to win at the border. We're going to win so much, you're going to be so sick and tired of winning, you're going to come to me and go 'Please, please, we can't win anymore.' You've heard this one. You'll say 'Please, Mr. President, we beg you sir, we don't want to win anymore. It's too much. It's not fair to everybody else.'" Trump said. "And I'm going to say 'I'm sorry, but we're going to keep winning, winning, winning. We're going to make America great again." [44]

In May 2106, candidate Donald Trump held a rally in Billings, Montana. The audience consisted mostly of white men who roared and cheered as he spoke in ways reminiscent of how warriors returning from battle were greeted in the days of tribal warfare. Trump was their avenger, a winner who had slayed the enemies and was on the journey to "Make America Great Again."

Trump's campaign slogan has the status trigger built into it: Making America great again meant restoring status that had been lost, a loss that felt like a mortal threat to the people in the room. Trump bypassed the crowd's conscious rationality by repeating the word "win" until the hyperbole of "we beg you sir, we don't want to win anymore" as a reasonable goal felt real. Winning felt attainable, and with winning would come a resurrection of the lost status, a reward that neurologically delivers more than jobs, healthcare, or pretty much anything else.

Trump doesn't rely just on the language of winning. He sets up the contest—the battle—that he has to fight in order to be a winner, and in creating his own rules for winning, he makes the win unchallengeable.

"When you go along and you have all these people running, it's the largest field," Trump said, describing his unexpected rise to presumptive Republican presidential nominee. He continued:

> I think it's the largest field. I don't know. I think it's the largest field. John, is that the largest field? Ask Campaign Carl. Is this the largest field ever to run? Please tell us. If Campaign Carl says it, it's true. Unless he's talking about me, understand no one knows more about politics.

Because it was "the largest field"—i.e., the biggest battle—the win was boosted by magnifying the scope of the battle. Trump's crowd cheered wildly, instinctively feeling their own status rise in being a supporter of this warrior who had slayed "the largest field" and was going to "Make America Great

Again" and restore the status they had lost, which they were certain they couldn't retrieve without this warrior.

Manipulators lie. Believers believe the lie.

In this fake reality of lies, everyone is traveling low roads to each other's brains. So, no one asks the high-road questions: "Why does it feel like we have lost status?" "Who did we lose our status to?" "When was the Great America to which we want to return?" "Was there actually real winning?" "Does any of this make rational sense?"

Once the fake reality is created, the manipulator can provide fake answers to these questions because the solution always rests within the manipulator. The crowds will believe the lies because the reward of increasing their status is irresistible.

Rational irrationality keeps this alternative reality intact. Facts and data can't dismantle this reality. Only the threat that supporting this warrior will reduce their status can make this fake reality vulnerable to extinction.

Rational Irrationality: Self-Interest

There are many ways in which rational irrationality manifests in the context of self-interest, but one particularly powerful manifestation occurs in how we tolerate and even enjoy cruelty and denigration of others in order to preserve our self-interest.

Since 2010, Dictionary.com has selected a word of the year as a "symbol of each year's most meaningful events and loop trends" to create "an opportunity for us to reflect on the language and ideas that represented each year." Dictionary.com's word for 2017: complicit. Dictionary.com's word for 2018: misinformation.

According to a representative at Dictionary.com, "Lookups of the word complicit increased by 300 percent in 2017 from 2016, notably driven by three news events—all related to the Trump family."

Complicit acts almost always reflect negative behavior. They are driven primarily by self-interest. Complicit acts also are a frequent mechanism through which manipulators encourage enabling behavior, and the acts are ones in which believers most easily engage.

Dictionary.com's word for 2016 was xenophobia. When you put xenophobia together with complicit, you have a pretty solid summary of the alternative reality created by Trump and of the self-interested behavior expressed by his supporters. And schadenfreude is one of Trump's favorite manipulation techniques to keep the alternative realities of his complicitly xenophobic world intact for his supporters.

Schadenfreude

Many malignant liars, like Trump, not only tell self-serving lies, but they also tell cruel self-serving lies because they instinctively get how schadenfreude works. Schadenfreude is the enjoyment we feel when we hear about someone else's misery. When we see people getting knocked down in any way, our brains see ourselves as rising in status to a point higher than them, thus triggering enjoyment in us and validating our sense of self as separate from the people being denigrated. Studies show that people who are insecure and afraid are more likely to experience schadenfreude than people who feel more in control because the lower someone's sense of self is, the more external validation they need to make sure their self-interests are important. For example, being envious of someone is a strong indicator of whether you would feel either schadenfreude or empathy when she suffers misfortune or embarrassment. Confident people who are not envious of others are more likely to offer to help someone when hearing of their misery instead of feeling a sense of enjoyment.

Researchers have found that "we can indeed take pleasure in the pain of others—particularly those we envy," and this is "so commonplace that scientists believe it must be a basic biological response in humans."[45]

While most of us feel schadenfreude when watching a rival lose against our favorite sports team or watching an opponent to our chosen candidate plummet in the polls, malignant liars use our schadenfreude tendencies to create clear us-versus-them distinctions, and, then, they poke fun at "them" to make "us" feel better about ourselves.

CNN Sucks

In late Summer 2018, Donald Trump held rallies across the United States to encourage Republican voters to get out and vote in the November midterm elections. He had many options as to how to spark voter enthusiasm, and he selected a mode that best suits his malignant liar tendencies: schadenfreude.

In order to trigger schadenfreude in his rally attendees, Trump first needed to create an us-versus-them distinction. It would be most effective to create a "them" that he could point to during his rallies. He picked the media as the schadenfreude target. Trump started defining the media as the elite, which looked down on his supporters, and as the rich and powerful, who had no idea what real Americans experienced. This echoed themes of his nomination acceptance speech at the Republican National Convention in July 2016, when he said:

> Big business, elite media, and major donors are lining up behind the campaign of my opponent because they know she will keep our rigged system in place. Remember: all of the people telling you that you can't have the country you want, are the same people telling you that I wouldn't be standing here tonight. No longer can we rely on those elites in media, and politics, who will say anything to keep a rigged system in place. Instead, we must choose to believe in America.[46]

Next he needed to make sure that his rally attendees knew that they are different from—better than—the media. In February 2017, he had tweeted: "The FAKE NEWS media (failing @nytimes, @NBCNews, @ABC, @CBS, @CNN) is not my enemy, it is the enemy of the American People!"[47] He followed that up in early 2018 with, "Just remember, what you are seeing and what you are reading is not what's happening ... Just stick with us, don't believe the crap you see from these people, the fake news." Soon thereafter, he tweeted: "The Fake News hates me saying that they are the Enemy of the People only because they know it's TRUE. I am providing a great service by explaining this to the American People. They purposely cause great division & distrust. They can also cause War! They are very dangerous & sick!"[48]

Without any evidence of what the media is doing that is fake, dangerous, or sick, the message from Trump is that the media—i.e., the elite "them" that don't care about real Americans—embody negative characteristics that should be shunned. This ironic message comes from a President who used to be a reality television star and who regularly seeks media attention and ratings. Trump sends a carefully mixed message to his rally attendees that allows him to revel in media attention while triggering schadenfreude for his supporters when he maligned the media.

At each of his rallies, Trump pointed out the media in the back of the room and derided them as "fake news" and "enemy of the people." With each rally, the crowd's enjoyment of seeing the media put down grew. At the end of the summer, the schadenfreude in disparaging the media was in full effect:

> In the video [of a Trump rally in Florida], a broad-shouldered man points out his "Fuck the media" shirt to the camera. A Santa Claus lookalike in a Hawaiian shirt and a red MAGA hat gives the camera the finger; a woman in a long pink-checked shirt does the same. A woman with expensive-looking blond highlights gives an elaborate "thumbs down" to the camera ... During [Jim] Acosta's live shot at the rally, the crowd behind him gleefully shouts "CNN sucks! CNN sucks!" and calls him a "traitor."[49]

Schadenfreude is easy to whip up in people, especially when lies are used to create us-versus-them distinctions that benefit the liar. But schadenfreude also can be countered with courageous human interaction that evokes empathy instead of animosity. After a particularly schadenfreude-laden Trump rally during which CNN reporter Jim Acosta was harassed, cursed at, and threatened, he approached two of the rally attendees to ask them why they were so angry at him. The couple, "identified as Merlin and Ilene, told the network's chief White House correspondent Wednesday evening that they were sorry for how they treated him at a rally in Tampa, Florida ... 'just wanted to apologize for flipping you off in Tampa. I got carried away,' Merlin said."[50]

Schadenfreude is real and powerful when deployed by malignant liars. But, like many of the manipulation tactics used by these liars, it is most real and powerful when the liars are actively keeping their lies alive.

Believers and the Complications of Politics

Within all of these contexts, there is a force of influence in how we process the world around us and respond to reality: politics. Our political perspectives—even if we are apolitical—are crucial filters through which we take in, process, interpret, and act on data. Neurobehavioral research has started providing us some insights as to how exactly these filters may work.

We've explored the amygdala, but in order to better understand the role that the amygdala plays in how we react to lies, we also need to understand the anterior cingulate cortex (ACC), a collar-shaped part of the brain located in the middle of the frontal lobe. The ACC has been found to be related to decision-making, socially driven interactions, and empathy-related responses. While the amygdala helps us escape danger, the ACC helps us understand and make sense of the world around us. Thinking back on the example of our ancient ancestors hearing rustling behind a bush, while their amygdalas helped them survive, it was their ACCs that helped them take some risks, figure out what was causing the rustling, and forge forward in spite of danger.

In 2011, researchers from the University College London Institute of Cognitive Neuroscience studied the brain scans of ninety healthy young adults who had self-reported their political leanings (conservative to liberal) and found that "greater liberalism was associated with increased gray matter volume in the anterior cingulate cortex, whereas greater conservatism was associated with increased volume of the right amygdala."

In several studies, psychologists and neurologists have consistently found that people who see themselves as conservative are more anxious, more easily frightened about the world around them, and more likely to want to maintain the status quo as a way to sustain stability and structure. Conservatives also are more likely to want clear and simple answers to perceived threats, even if the threats are too complex to be distilled into simple answers. In 2011, Paul Nail, a social psychologist at University of Central Arkansas, found that "when people feel safe and secure, they become more liberal; when they feel threatened, they become more conservative." Nail and his colleagues found that regardless of whether people considered themselves liberal or conservative, everyone became more conservative after the terrorist attacks in September 2011.

Similarly, in 2012, Philip Tetlock from the Wharton School of Business found that conservatives are:

> less tolerant of compromise; see the world in "us" versus "them" terms; are more willing to use force to gain an advantage; are "more prone to rely on simple (good versus bad) evaluative rules in interpreting policy issues;" are "motivated to punish violators of social norms" (e.g., deviations from traditional norms of sexuality or responsible behavior) and to deter free riders. [51]

Other researchers, including Jonathan Haidt, University of Virginia; Nicholas Winter, University of Virginia; and Ravi Iyer, University of Southern California, systematically organized and analyzed thousands of online public opinion surveys to create rough outlines of the two political coalitions that exist in the United States: "the first, a socially and economically dominant coalition on the right; the second, a coalition on the left composed of relatively disadvantaged (subdominant) voters in alliance with relatively well-educated, well-off, culturally liberal professionals ('information workers,' 'symbol analysts,' 'creatives,' 'knowledge workers,' etc.)." The following areas of greatest differentiation between the two coalitions sheds new light on how we understand our political world, our political speech, and our own perspectives as political beings:

1. War, Peace, Violence, Empathy With the World

   On key questions and statements in this category, liberals scored high, conservatives low: "I believe peace is extremely important"; "Understanding, appreciation, and protection for the welfare of all people and for nature"; "One of the worst things a person could do is hurt a defenseless animal"; "How close do you feel to people all over the world?"

On other key questions in this area, conservatives scored high, and liberals low: "War is sometimes the best way to solve a conflict"; "There is nothing wrong in getting back at someone who has hurt you."

2. 'Crime and Punishment; Moral Elasticity; Authority

Again, on some questions in this category, liberals scored high, conservatives low: "I believe that offenders should be provided with counseling to aid in their rehabilitation"; "What is ethical varies from one situation and society to another."

On other questions, conservatives scored high and liberals low: "People should not do things that are disgusting, even if no one is harmed"; "Respect for authority is something all children need to learn"; "I believe that 'an eye for an eye' is the correct philosophy behind punishing offenders"; "The 'old-fashioned ways' and 'old-fashioned values' still show the best way to live"; "It feels wrong when . . . a person commits a crime and goes unpunished."

3. The Poor, Redistribution, Fairness:

Liberal high, conservative low: "It feels wrong when . . . an employee who needs their job, is fired"; "I think it's morally wrong that rich children inherit a lot of money while poor children inherit nothing"; "I often have tender, concerned feelings for people less fortunate than me."

Conservative high, liberal low: "[I place a high value on] safety, harmony, and stability of society, of relationships, and of self"; "[It's desirable when] employees [who] contribute more to the success of the company receive a larger share"; "[I value] social status and prestige, control or dominance over people and resources."

4. Morals, Hedonism, Self-Fulfillment, Hierarchy:

Liberals high, conservatives low: "I see myself as someone who . . . is original, comes up with new ideas"; "Pleasure or sensuous gratification for oneself"; "What is ethical varies from one situation and society to another."

Conservative high, liberal low: "If certain groups stayed in their place, we would have fewer problems;" "People should be loyal to their family members, even when they have done something wrong;" "Respect, commitment, and acceptance of the customs that traditional culture provide"; "[I favor] restraint of actions, inclinations, and impulses likely to upset or harm others and violate social expectations or norms."

If you experienced different emotions as you read the different responses above, it says more about your political mindset than about anything that is absolutely right or absolutely wrong. It is difficult to not see our own mindsets as right and the other side's mindset as wrong.

In *The Righteous Mind: Why Good People Are Divided by Politics and Religion*, Jonathan Haidt advocates for both sides to better value the other side in order to create a society that is at its strongest. Haidt wants:

> the left to acknowledge that the right's emphasis on laws, institutions, customs and religion is valuable. Conservatives recognize that democracy is a huge achievement and that maintaining the social order requires imposing constraints on people. Liberal values, on the other hand, also serve important roles: ensuring that the rights of weaker members of society are respected; limiting the harmful effects, such as pollution, that corporations sometimes pass on to others; and fostering innovation by supporting diverse ideas and ways of life.

We cannot have diversity and innovation without stability and order, but stability and order cannot help us stay competitive and move forward as a nation without diversity and innovation. We need both those with stronger amygdalas and those with stronger ACCs to work together to create a better world because neither is absolutely right or wrong, and both need the other more than they like to acknowledge.

That said, those who have a more conservative mindset are more vulnerable to malignant liars' lies because malignant liars primarily use fear as a way to get what they want and to get away with their lies. People with conservative mindsets can more easily become believers for malignant liars because their focus on fears makes them easier to manipulate.

Malignant liars rely heavily on believers, and believers are vulnerable to believing manipulators' lies for a multitude of reasons. When believers believe the lies, they are lured into the fake worlds created by the liars, and they believe the fake dangers and the fake fixes wholeheartedly. Believers believe that if these fake dangers are slayed with the fake fixes, their lives will change for the better, and they are cheering for the manipulator to be successful in order to make their own lives better.

Manipulators need believers—and the more the merrier. However, believers alone don't sustain the worlds that the manipulators want to exploit; they also need enablers. Enablers don't always believe the lies, but they help the manipulators maintain the lies because they don't believe they otherwise will be able to access certain opportunities without the manipulators. Most enablers would never lie prolifically like the malignant liars, but they are happy to vicariously claim the spoils of the lies.

Chapter 6:
The Enablers

Enablers don't necessarily believe the lies, but they help liars maintain malignant lies because enablers feel that their own lives will be worse off if the liars' lies crumble around them.

Remember my client Jim, who lied to us so much that we ended up having to fire him? A couple of years after we had severed our relationship with him, I ran into someone who had worked with him. I didn't know her very well, but she hugged me tightly when she saw me, and she started crying. She told me how terrible she and her colleagues had felt when they would get on the phone and agree with his lies.

"He lied all the time. It was terrible how we had to lie for him. I was just so scared that he would make it hard for me to get another job, so I stayed," she told me as she cried.

I asked her what made her finally leave. She told me that Jim had started lying about her to the Board of Directors, and she finally realized that she would lose her job if she didn't quit. So she did.

Enabling Madoff's Madness

In December 2008, after the news had broken about Bernie Madoff's Ponzi scheme, the Securities Investor Protection Corporation (SIPC) installed Irving H. Picard as the Trustee for liquidating Madoff's assets so that investors could recoup their losses. Picard filed thousands of lawsuits to recover more than $90 billion. In many of these suits, Picard directly called out financial institutions and funds as Madoff's enablers.

In a suit against JP Morgan Chase, Picard and his team said that JP Morgan "not only should have known that a fraud was being perpetrated, they did know." He added that:

> JP Morgan's bankers could see that money customers deposited into Bernard L. Madoff Investment Securities LLC's (BLMIS) main account was not being used to purchase or sell securities … they could see that it was merely transferred to other customers, in patterns serving no legitimate business purpose. They could see that Madoff's regulatory filings were materially inconsistent with BLMIS's actual finances … they allowed the fraud to continue.[52]

Bloomberg, after its analysis of Madoff's financials, found dozens of enablers, such as fund marketers like Access International, middlemen like Robert Jaffe and J. Ezra Merkin, and feeder funds like Fairfield Greenwich, which funneled $25 billion of their clients' money to Madoff while looking the other way. Picard and his team sued all the enablers to recover what they could for those who suffered devastating financial losses in Madoff's scheme. As a result, firms like Fairfield Greenwich are folding.

So, why would these enablers take these risks, which could possibly destroy their businesses and reputations and possibly land them in jail? Money, fame, lavish lifestyles, feeling special, the thrill of getting away with something, security. While these aren't the only motivators for enablers, they cover the majority of the reasons why enablers enable.

The enablers were supposed to be some of the checks on Madoff's lies; instead, they became Madoff's salespeople and cover stories. As long as the vicarious spoils were flowing into their pockets, the enablers looked the other way.

Enabling Trump's Crowd-Size Distortions

On January 21, 2017, the day after his inauguration as the 45th President of the United States, Donald J. Trump launched his presidency by claiming that

> the media had misrepresented the number of people attending his inauguration. Trump spoke at CIA headquarters and said that "one of the networks" had shown "an empty field," while he saw a crowd that "looked like a million-and-a-half people" and "went all the way back to the Washington Monument." Trump claimed that "we caught [the media] in a beauty, and I think they're going to pay a big price."[53]

Sean Spicer, the White House press secretary at the time, provided a statement to the White House Press Corps in which he asserted that: "photographs of the inaugural proceedings were intentionally framed in a way, in one particular tweet, to minimize the enormous support that had gathered on the National Mall ... This was the largest audience to ever witness an inauguration—period—both in person and around the globe."[54]

After multiple analyses of crowd sizes from President Barack Obama's inauguration in 2009 and Trump's inauguration in 2017 incontrovertibly illustrated that both Trump and Spicer had lied, the Trump administration did not let the lie go. Counselor to the President Kellyanne Conway appeared on NBC's *Meet the Press* the next day, and the host, Chuck Todd, asked her why "the President asked the White House Press Secretary to come out in front of the podium for the first time and utter a falsehood?" Conway shrugged her shoulders and said, "Don't be so overly dramatic about it, Chuck. What—You're saying it's a falsehood. And they're giving Sean Spicer, our press secretary, gave alternative facts to that."[55]

The Cambridge dictionary defines a fact as "something known to have happened or to exist," fiction as "a false report or statement that you pretend is true," and a lie as "to say something that is not true in order to deceive."

Facts separate truth from fiction; intent to deceive separates fiction from a lie. Trump, Spicer, and Conway all lied, but Trump was the malignant liar whose lies Spicer and Conway were enabling. Enablers don't create new lies; they offer twisted explanations and justifications in their attempts to validate the malignant liar's original lies.

Spicer and Conway worked for Trump, and they both were senior advisors to one of the most powerful people on the planet. They were enabling his lies, but the enabling was not rooted in believing Trump's lies; the enabling was rooted in believing that Trump's success (however he achieved it) was critical for their own success.

Enabling Nassar's Abuses

In 1986, Larry Nassar was hired as an athletic trainer for the USA Gymnastics medical staff, and in 1993, he matriculated from Michigan State University with an osteopathic medical degree to become Dr. Larry Nassar. In 1997, Nassar became the team physician for USA Gymnastics and an assistant professor at Michigan State University.

According to the various civil suits, criminal prosecutions, and witness impact statements filed against Nassar, the following are just a few proven allegations on his extensive timeline of sexual abuse and assault of young female athletes:[56]

- In 1997, a gymnast's parent files a complaint with the Olympic team's coach, John Geddert, about Nassar's treatments. Geddert does nothing.

- In 1998, Nassar sexually abuses six-year-old Kyle Stephens, a daughter of good friends, and convinces Kyle's parents that Kyle is making it up.

- In 1999, a "Michigan State cross country athlete tells athletic program staff she was sexually assaulted by Nassar while receiving treatment for an injured hamstring, according to her lawsuit filed in 2017. According to the athlete, her concerns were dismissed by a coach who said Nassar was 'an Olympic doctor' and 'knew what he was doing.'"

- In 2000, "Michigan State softball player Tiffany Thomas Lopez tells three university athletic trainers and one staff member that Nassar was sexually inappropriate during medical treatments ... Lopez says she was told that 'she was fortunate to receive the best medical care possible from a world-renowned doctor.'"

- In 2004, a "17-year-old visits Nassar for treatment for scoliosis. After Nassar abuses the young woman during the visit, she and her mother report the incident to the Meridian Township Police Department. Nassar defends his actions to police as valid medical treatment, using a PowerPoint presentation as supporting evidence. No charges are made. A redacted police report related to the incident was released on Jan. 30, 2017."

- In 2014, "Michigan State graduate Amanda Thomashow reports to Dr. Jeff Kovan of the MSU Sports Medicine Clinic that she was sexually assaulted by Nassar during a medical examination to treat a hip injury she sustained in high school. University president Lou Anna K. Simon is made aware of a Title IX complaint, and that a police report had been filed against an unnamed physician. Nassar continues to treat patients for 16 months during the MSU Police Department investigation."

- In 2015, USA Gymnastics fires Nassar; in 2016, Michigan State University also fires him.

- In 2016, Nassar is "indicted on federal child pornography charges," and "eighteen women file a lawsuit in federal court against Nassar, Michigan State, USA Gymnastics, and Twistars Gymnastics Club."

- In early 2017, Michigan suspends Nassar's license to practice medicine, and "Michigan State gymnastics coach Kathie Klages is suspended after court records show two women say she discouraged them from filing sexual assault complaints against Nassar in the late 1990s. Klages retires from Michigan State the following day."

- By the end of 2017, "twenty-three more women and girls join a federal lawsuit against Nassar. There are now over 100 complaints against him." Nassar pleads guilty to the child pornography charge in federal court, seven counts of "first-degree criminal sexual misconduct in Ingham County Circuit Court as part of a plea agreement," and "three counts of first-degree criminal sexual conduct in Eaton County Circuit Court as part of plea agreement."

- In December 2017, Nassar "is sentenced to 60 years in prison on federal child pornography charges."

- In January 2018, 156 women read Victim Impact Statements during an eight-day sentencing hearing for Nassar in Ingham County Circuit Court in Michigan.

- In January 2018, "Judge Rosemarie Aquilina sentences Larry Nassar to 40 to 175 years in prison on seven counts of criminal sexual assault. During sentencing Judge Aquilina states that her sentence will begin after Nassar completed his 60-year federal sentence for child pornography."

- In February 2018, "Judge Janice Cunningham sentences Larry Nassar to 40 to 125 years in prison on three charges of criminal sexual misconduct in Eaton County Court."

After more than twenty years of complaints against Nassar, he was sentenced to a prison term that will ensure he spends the rest of his life in prison. But Nassar did not terrorize young girls for more than two decades without help. From USA Gymnastics to Michigan State University, Nassar's enablers helped create a context of impunity in which the doctor could continue his assaults and abuses and lie about them to preserve his livelihood and his life.

Moreover, his enablers were not held accountable until after his sentencing. Eventually, every member of the USA Gymnastics Board of

Directors resigned, and John Geddert, USA Gymnastics Women's National Team coach, was suspended. Michigan State University's athletic director, Mark Hollis, and president, Lou Anna K. Simon, resigned. The United States Olympic Committee has warned USA Gymnastics that the sport could be decertified if it doesn't fix what led to it enabling of Nassar. And, Kathy Clages, the Michigan State University gymnastics coach to whom many of the victims had reported the abuse, was charged with lying to the police about not knowing about the abuses.

Nassar consistently lied when initially and periodically confronted with his crimes. His enablers didn't necessarily believe him, but they made it possible for his abuses and lies to continue.

Believers are only guilty of being gullible, but enablers can actually be culpable for the actions they take to protect the liar and cover up the lies. Without enablers, the liars cannot survive long enough to amass a critical following.

The Coattail Riders

Believers believe the lies, and enablers provide the liars with the cover they need to survive and thrive. Coattail riders are those who legitimize and validate what the liars are doing by periodically criticizing some of the liars' behaviors and pretending to seek the truth while amassing personal gains from the lies. Coattail riders don't get dirty with lies or coverups; instead, they leverage the context that the liar has created to get what they want.

Evangelical Leaders

Hypocrisy has its own elegant symmetry.
—Julie Metz

Evangelical Christians subscribe to many of the beliefs and practices of most Christian denominations, but, historically, Evangelicals have embraced a more socially traditional and politically conservative perspective that is deeply rooted in literal interpretations of the Bible.

In the 1990s, Evangelical leaders decried the moral decay they believed President Bill Clinton was ushering into American politics through his extramarital affairs and sexual promiscuity. They strongly advocated that the President of the United States needed to be an unambiguous moral leader in order for our country to prosper.[57] A few years later, these same Evangelical leaders embraced Donald Trump, a twice-divorced, thrice-married adulterer who had bragged about sexually assaulting women, as chosen by God to lead this country.[58]

Roughly 81 percent of Evangelicals voted for Trump, and many of them reported that they did so even though they did not really want to vote for him. In 2016, the Pew Research Center found "that while 78 percent of self-identified white evangelical voters planned to vote for Trump, 45 percent were mainly voting against Hillary Clinton and only 30 percent were voting for Trump himself."[59] Even as Evangelicals touted the importance of each person living up to full Christian ideals, they were willing to support for the highest elected office in this country a man who not only did not live up to the ideals they held dear but violated many of them frequently. As *Christianity Today* reported:

> In what would have been anathema to evangelicals in the 1990s who saw leadership as intimately connected to character, evangelicals today display a stunning pragmatism regarding behavior. In our research, this fact became strikingly clear: Of those with an opinion, 3 out of 4 evangelicals by belief agree that a political leader's personal life does not need to line up with Christian teaching in order for Christians to benefit.[60]

So, lying and cheating (two of the Ten Commandments) are bad, but if a liar and a cheat will get you what you want, it's okay. As Sarah Jones wrote in *The New Republic*, "Evangelicals know Trump is a liar. They just don't care."[61]

Even as Evangelicals tout the importance of the Gospel guiding all behaviors, "Evangelical activists are fine with Trump's lies because they grasp the bargain they've made for power."[62] They don't believe Trump's lies, and they don't enable his behavior by justifying the lies or explaining them away, but they do swallow their moral distaste to vote for him because the ride to power on Trump's coattails gets them what they want, even if they don't care for the man whose coattails they are riding.

Coattail riders keep their hands clean but use an elegant hypocrisy to continue to support malignant liars that they may disdain and rely upon in equal parts to secure the gains they are seeking.

Taking on Malignant Liars and Their Teams

Malignant liars rely on their believers, enablers, and coattail riders to keep their lies alive while they pilfer what they want from the world around them. The more powerful the liars are, the more formidable their teams look. It can be frustrating and unnerving to consider the vast systems of complicity that help liars get away with lying, but the good news is that we don't have to dismantle complex systems in order to take down liars.

The systems are formidable, but in reality, they are houses of cards that can implode with the right external pressure. The multibillion-dollar Enron fiasco came down through the efforts of one whistleblower. The "American Dad" narrative that Bill Cosby had spent decades building dissolved after one woman came forward with her story of being sexually assaulted by him. Harvey Weinstein's empire was breached by one employee's memo.

Winning against liars—especially powerful liars—is a classic David-versus-Goliath battle. We can be smaller and less powerful than the liars, but with the right stone slung in the right direction at the right angle, the giant can be vanquished.

Section III:
Winning Against Liars ...
Without Losing Your Mind

Winning Against Liars

Winning against liars is a tricky endeavor because, in order to win, we first have to define what it means to win for us. While outing the liar and proving him a charlatan are laudable social justice or feel-good goals, they can pull you deeper into and trap you in a liar's game where the only winning possible is for the liar.

What does winning mean when dealing with a malignant liar? Here are a few quotes from women and men I have interviewed and worked with about how they finally defined winning against the malignant liar in their lives:

> It had been almost a year of dealing with a vendor we couldn't fire who lied constantly and created ridiculous amounts of work for my business unit. We tried everything from cajoling to threatening to giving more work to their competitors, but they were just too powerful in our industry, and we would lose too much business if we just fired them, so we had to redefine for ourselves what winning meant to us. Your idea of a malignant liar resonated with us, and we decided to treat this vendor like something that should be quarantined, so we created a special tactical unit to only deal with this vendor. The vendor's bullshit would be contained, and it wouldn't infect all of us all the time. There were four people in this unit, and the rest of us treated them like heroes. We would buy them coffee every morning. People brought in bagels and donuts for them. Anyone making an afternoon Starbucks run would make sure that they got orders from this unit. The unit's only responsibility is dealing

with this vendor, and we've decided that people will do "tours" in this unit of twelve months at a time. Once we isolated this vendor in this way, it became a game, and the war metaphors have even become funny. We even got camouflage mugs for them with their names on it and "Special Tactical Unit" under their names. The vendor still lies all the time, but we aren't suffering from it like we used to.

—Alexis

My coworker—he and I were peers—was a toxic liar. He lied about everything. He was that guy that had a picture of a model from a magazine in a frame in his office and told everyone that was his girlfriend. He lied to the person who is our direct boss. He constantly took credit for my work, talked down to me in meetings, and just went behind my back to my boss with lies about me. When I went to talk to my boss about him, she told me that she knew that he was lying but that I needed to find a way to deal with him and stand up for myself. I was angry about that at first because I felt like she should be doing more to help me, but I realized that other people on our team wouldn't respect me if she bailed me out. I thought a lot about what winning meant to me. After rejecting, you know, really fun ideas like punching him in his nose and spreading malicious rumors about him, I decided that winning meant detaching my emotions in dealing with him so I could always respond with deadpan seriousness. I'm a really emotional person, so I took an acting class. I know that's hilarious, but the acting class helped me think of me and him as actors in an awful play. I knew his tired old lines, and I could write my lines. It became something silly to do instead of stress to deal with. I told one of my other coworkers about it, and we would have script revision sessions that were rolling on the floor funny. Once my emotions were out of it, I figured out how to make sure my boss knew what I was working on and how to give her enough information so that she always had the information she needed to ask him tough questions when he went behind my back.

—*Lydia*

The only way to win was to walk away. I was at a firm where a senior person constantly made sexually offensive and demeaning comments, but he always did it when it was just me and him alone. I complained, but I was told that it was just too much of a "he say, she say" situation to take action against him. He was this way with a couple of other women, too. Even though there was more than just me, he lied about it every time someone complained, and the firm kept apologizing because there was no "evidence." He even joked with me one time about how I had complained and how naïve I was that I thought anyone would believe me over him. I could have filed a suit and done other things like that. But, in the end, the best thing was for me to walk away. I have three young kids and working with him was taking away energy I needed for my kids. And, legal action would have done the same thing. I left the firm. Initially, it felt like he had won: He got away with being a sexist asshole, right? But, I realized that once I left, I was free to be honest about what had happened. I had lunch with one of the leaders of the firm and told him exactly why I had left and I told him that I was going to be honest about my experiences there with everyone I talked to. He offered to hire me back and in a different area, but I declined. I'm happy where I am. Now, I'm not one of those zen people who will say that I'm glad I went through that because it led me to a better place, but I do like where I am.

—*Jillian*

I don't think of it as winning. I think of it as doing the right thing. I know it's probably different for me because I'm a man and the liar was also a man. He was a little senior to me but not so much that I was out of line in calling him out by asking him direct questions every time he opened his mouth. I'm not saying he lied every single time he said something, but he lied enough that I questioned everything. We are in a business where details matter, and I did feel like it was the right thing to do to ask someone to back up what they said with details. He complained to senior people that I was confrontational and difficult to work with. I was told to go easier on him, but I didn't. He eventually left. My female colleagues have told me repeatedly that I was able to deal with it the way I did because I was a man and that they would have been fired if they had dealt with this guy the same way. I think that's a valid point. I'm trying to be the type of leader where people know that doing the right thing is better for the whole team.

—Patrick

Alexis, Lydia, Jillian, and Patrick did not arrive at their eventual definitions of winning against the liars in their lives easy or simple ways. Each of them struggled through the frustrating journeys of realizing they were being lied to, recognizing that the lies were not going to stop, and trying many different ways of dealing with the liars before accepting that the wins against liars needed to be practical wins that served their own needs, not moral victories that outed the liars or extracted confessions from them in some way.

Play *Your* Game to Win

All of the research on outsmarting liars points to avoiding the liar's game and playing your own game to win, which means:

- recognizing and avoiding the insanity traps inherent in dealing with malignant liars, and

- knowing the game you want to play, defining what winning looks like for you, and identifying the people who could be on your team.

As tempting as it is—and it is very tempting—it is an exercise in futility to out a liar just for the sake of outing the liar. Malignant liars are much more committed to maintaining their lies than we ever will be to exposing them. The thought of proving a liar wrong with a major reveal of having the liar confess because of an aha! moment is a tantalizing one, but the probability of exhausting yourself in the pursuit is significantly greater than any successful reveal or aha! moment.

As Alexis's, Lydia's, Jillian's, and Patrick's stories demonstrate, there is no one way to win against a malignant liar, but there is a way that works best for you. Winning against a malignant liar is about finding that way that works for you. In order to find that way and define the game you want to play, you first have to avoid losing your mind.

Chapter 7:
Recognize and Avoid the
Insanity Traps

Insanity is often the logic of an accurate mind overtasked.
—Oliver Wendell Holmes Sr.

Malignant liars create worlds where facts, logic, and reason have been excised with deliberate care; thus, the work of sticking to facts when liars weave fact-less fantasies can induce insanity. You should take the time to understand the malignant liars—the games they play, the fears they tap into to create believers, and the fears that drive their lying ways—but you also should pivot quickly from understanding them to neutralizing them. The gravitational pull of malignant liars can be quite strong, and attempts to rationally understand the irrationality behind why the liars are lying or why people are believing the lies can lead to insanity.

Insanity Trap #1:
Trying to Prove the Liar Is Lying

While average liars like most of us are shamed or guilted when our lies are proven to be false, malignant liars do not care about any of that. They will not stop lying just because their lies have been proven wrong. They are not lying to be believed by everyone; they are lying to get what they want. They need only enough believers, enablers, and coattail riders to get what they want. They do not care if their lies are proven to be lies as long as they are able to continue getting what they want.

The way out of Insanity Trap # 1 is to focus on the facts. Write down the facts. Do not allow anyone else to blur or pervert the facts.

Facts are provable things about which everyone everywhere can reach the same conclusion. Facts are the building blocks of truths, but truths can extend beyond facts into subjective interpretations of experiences. Truths rely on facts and are accurate reflections of reality; however, there can be more than one reflection of any particular reality. For example, a temperature of 85° Fahrenheit is a measurable fact: temperature in that moment = 85°.

Although the temperature is incontrovertible, the concept of heat is subjective. If someone says that it is hot outside when it is 85°, the statement is true for that person: hot = 85°. But different people can define hot differently. So, hot may equal 95° degrees for people who are used to 85° temperatures, and hot may equal 75° for people who are used to 55° temperatures. Both conclusions can be true.

Truth is a dynamic narrative that can change as some facts become obsolete and new facts emerge. Truth is rooted in facts but also includes interpretations, inferences, and opinions to build a story that people believe. If a story is accepted, the truth is believed.

Facts are proven. Truth is believed.

Similar to a truth, a lie also is a story that can be believed (or not); unlike truth, however, a lie does not rely on facts. Lies are narratives created by people who intentionally mislead by pretending that their narratives are relying on facts when they know they are not. It is critical to stress "intentionally" in defining lies because there is a difference between people simply being wrong (saying things that are not facts and/or truth without any intention to deceive) and lying, which requires the intention to deceive. People who are wrong believe what they are saying is a fact and/or truth. People who are lying do not believe what they are saying is a fact and/or truth; they do want others to believe that what they are saying is a fact and/or truth.

Each of us faces malignant liars in the world around us whose lies spin realities that damage us, our loved ones, and our communities, lies that constrain our abilities to be free, happy, peaceful, and safe. The battles against these malignant liars are real battles with real consequences, and they can't be won by pitting lies against truths. We cannot play against malignant liars the way we do against benign liars. Challenging the "truth" of what they are saying works with benign liars; that tactic doesn't work against malignant liars who are not anchored to the truth at all.

Malignant liars are playing a game where they tell stories that sound and feel like "truth" to their believers. In understanding the game they are playing, we realize that the only way to stay sane when engaging with malignant the liars who tell these lies is to fight back with facts.

That's exactly what journalist Peter Alexander did in February 2017 in a press conference when Donald Trump lied and said, "I guess it [2016 Presidential election] was the biggest electoral college win since Ronald Reagan."[1] Peter Alexander responded with facts, "you said today that you had the biggest electoral margin since Ronald Reagan, with 304, 306 electoral votes. The fact that President Obama got 365 ..."[2]

Trump immediately interrupted him to say, "Well I'm talking about Republican." Peter Alexander responded with the fact that George H. W. Bush had won 426 electoral votes in 1988, and Trump backed down with, "Well, I don't know, I was given that information. I was given that. We had a very big margin."[3]

By focusing on facts, Peter Alexander succeeded in getting Trump to back down from his original claim, but the truth is that Trump's believers may continue to believe what he initially said regardless of Alexander's introduction of contradictory facts into the exchange. Peter Alexander won against Trump in that moment because his job as a journalist requires him to win against lies like this, but if Alexander or anyone else wanted Trump's believers to abandon their belief in what Trump initially said, they would be falling into Insanity Trap #2.

Insanity Trap #2: Trying to Get the Liar's Believers to Stop Believing

As we explored in the section about a liar's believers, the need to believe a liar's lies is an irrational one resistant to facts, logic, and reason. As Michael Ende writes in *The Neverending Story*, "When it comes to controlling human beings there is no better instrument than lies. Because, you see, humans live by beliefs. And beliefs can be manipulated. The power to manipulate beliefs is the only thing that counts." Trying to change belief with facts, logic, and/or reason is not only an exercise in futility but a surefire journey to madness.

Many malignant liars will have their base of believers, and neither understanding why believers believe nor changing these believers' beliefs is necessary in defeating the liar. Winning against malignant liars requires us to make peace with the fact that liars have their believers, and the believers' ardor often can make the liars look like they are winning with their lies.

In order to outsmart liars, you have to focus on the lies and how they affect your life; you cannot focus on the liars or their believers.

When the U.S. Government wanted to take on liars like Clark Stanley, the original snake oil salesman, it didn't focus its efforts on trying to prove that he was lying or on trying to convince his believers that their beliefs were not rational. The United States passed the Pure Food and Drug Act and charged scientists with testing food and drug to make sure that labels were factually accurate with the ingredients. They found that Stanley's snake oil had no snake oil in it, and the products were banned. Stanley paid a fine, and although his believers didn't stop believing Stanley, his lies could no longer drain their wallets.

Insanity Trap #3:
Trying to Get the Liar's Enablers to Admit That the Liar Is Lying

The liar's enablers do not believe the liar's lies. They know the liar is lying, but they are invested in maintaining the façade of the lies for their own personal gain. Trying to hold them accountable by proving the liar is lying doesn't work because their enabling words and actions already have taken into account that the liar is lying. The enablers' defense against your efforts to hold them accountable is to insist that the liar is telling the truth. This pushes you back to the first insanity trap: trying to prove the liar is lying.

You should avoid falling into the trap of trying to hold the liar's enablers accountable for enabling the liar. Instead, you can ensure that the enablers are so closely tied to the liar that their desire to continue to enable the liar diminishes as you fight the liar with facts. As the enablers slowly distance themselves from the liar, the liar's ability to continue lying also diminishes, as does the liar's power.

We previously explored the National Rifle Association as a malignant liar of the institutional sort. Let's take another look at them through the relationship between the NRA and their primary enablers: legislators who have taken NRA-funded donations. These lawmakers have sponsored and passed laws that favor the NRA's positions that support having as few regulations on gun sales as possible despite the devastating tragedies caused by a lack of common-sense gun regulations. The legislators didn't necessarily believe the NRA's lies; rather, campaign contributions flowing the NRA after they purported to believe them were incentive enough to create laws based on lies ... until a group of teenage survivors of a horrible mass shooting at a school tied the enablers so closely to the NRA while the teenagers fought the NRA with facts that the enablers slowly but surely stopped enabling.

The NRA Neutralized

We previously explored the power that the NRA wields to ensure that buying guns has become deeply intertwined with protecting ourselves and our families. So powerful has the NRA become that it has continued to be successful in advocating for gun sales even while Americans are being killed in mass shootings due to the increasing prevalence of guns.

Gun law reform advocates and families of loved ones slain by guns have been actively and arduously fighting against the NRA—and the legislators they support—for decades, although to no avail. In spite of horrific mass shootings in America, such as the five worst noted below, the NRA has continued to get its way with limited restrictions in gun buying and stockpiling laws:

- **58 killed: October 1, 2017, Las Vegas, Nevada**—Stephen Paddock sprayed gunfire into a crowd of 22,000 concertgoers, killing 58 people and injuring almost 500.

- **49 killed: June 12, 2016, Orlando, Florida**—Omar Saddiqui Mateen opened fire inside a gay nightclub, killing 49 people and injuring more than 50.

- **32 killed: April 16, 2007, Virginia Tech in Blacksburg**—Seung-Hui Cho kills 32 people in two locations and wounds multiple others on campus.

- **27 killed: December 14, 2012, Sandy Hook Elementary School in Newtown, Connecticut**—Adam Lanza kills 20 children between the ages of 6 and 7 as well as 6 adults from school staff and faculty.

- **25 and an unborn child, November 5, 2017, Sutherland Springs, Texas**—Devin Patrick Kelley starts shooting in a small church, killing 25 people and an unborn child and wounding 20 others.

The NRA and its legislative enablers sent their thoughts and prayers to the victims of the above tragedies, but no one actually did anything to change the laws or regulations that allowed the above to happen.

146

Then February 14, 2018, happened. On that day, Nikolas Cruz walked into Marjory Stoneman Douglas High School in Parkland, Florida, and killed seventeen students and staff and wounded another seventeen. The images of students walking out of the high school with hands above their heads and tears running down their faces were devastating, and the "thoughts and prayers" reprise began.

Legislators bemoaned the tragedy as news media covered yet another story of yet another mass shooting in America. Unlike the other tragedies after which survivors shared their heartbreaking pain, the survivors of Marjory Stoneman Douglas High School shared their rage, and they targeted their rage at the NRA by closely linking the NRA with their legislative enablers and then going after the NRA with facts.

On February 17, 2018, Emma Gonzalez, one of the students who survived the shooting, gave a fiery speech in which she said:

> *If the President wants to come up to me and tell me to my face that it was a terrible tragedy and how it should never have happened and maintain telling us how nothing is going to be done about it, I'm going to happily ask him how much money he received from the National Rifle Association [...] You want to know something? It doesn't matter, because I already know. Thirty million dollars. And divided by the number of gunshot victims in the United States in the one and one-half months in 2018 alone, that comes out to being $5,800. Is that how much these people are worth to you, Trump [...] To every politician who is taking donations from the NRA, shame on you. Republican Senator Chuck Grassley of Iowa was the sole sponsor on this bill that stops the FBI from performing background checks on people adjudicated to be mentally ill and now he's stating for the record, "Well, it's a shame the FBI isn't doing background checks on these mentally ill people." Well, duh. You took that opportunity away last year.*
>
> *Politicians who sit in their gilded House and Senate seats funded by the NRA telling us nothing could have been done to prevent this,*

we call BS. They say tougher guns laws do not decrease gun violence. We call BS. They say a good guy with a gun stops a bad guy with a gun. We call BS. They say guns are just tools like knives and are as dangerous as cars. We call BS. They say no laws could have prevented the hundreds of senseless tragedies that have occurred. We call BS. That us kids don't know what we're talking about, that we're too young to understand how the government works. We call BS. If you agree, register to vote. Contact your local Congresspeople. Give them a piece of your mind.[4]

By calling out the politicians as the NRA's enablers and going after the NRA with facts, Emma Gonzalez and her classmates began an erosion of the legislative enabling of the NRA, which was foundational to the NRA's ability to keep lying.

One of the ways in which the NRA codified the enabling it received from legislators is that it graded legislators based on how much they supported the NRA's legislative agenda. The grades also translated into how much money the NRA gave to their enablers. The grades and the campaign contributions incentivized lawmakers to legislate in accordance with the NRA's wishes even though they knew that the data presented by the NRA to the public consists of one malignant lie after another. As *The Washington Post* reported in February 2018:

> One of the ways that the National Rifle Association exerts influence over elected officials is by giving them letter-grade ratings on gun issues. It's a shorthand for gun-rights voters in the way that the D or R next to a politician's name is a shorthand for voters in general. If a candidate has an A grade, it's a stamp of approval from the nation's preeminent gun advocacy organization.[5]

When the shooting at Marjory Stoneman Douglas happened, 8 members of Congress had received $1 million or more from the NRA, 39 had received $100,000 or more, and 128 had received $25,000 or more.[6] And all of these members of Congress received an A grade from the NRA and voted against every legislation that the NRA opposed regardless of how many of their own constituents had been killed by gun violence.

The lying and the enabling of the lying had been clearly connected, and the student activists did not back down. They organized "March for Our Lives," which drew a record-breaking 800,000 people to Washington, D.C., and millions more in cities across the country and around the world. Then the student activists organized people to get out and vote, and they asked people to vote for lawmakers who had earned F grades from the NRA.

As the students' voices became louder, the NRA's voice grew quieter. Suddenly, it became more disadvantageous for legislators to enable the NRA than it was to distance themselves from the organization. For the first time since the NRA started grading politicians, politicians started asking the NRA to not publish their grades. In June 2018, the NRA pulled all the old grades from their website and said they were no longer making their grades public. In the 2018 midterm elections, more NRA-backed candidates lost their seats in the U.S. House of Representatives than they had in the past twenty-five years.

As legislators realized that it was no longer in their political best interests to enable the NRA, they slowly backed away from the NRA. Without the support of its enablers, the NRA can still lie all it wants, but the ability of those lies to affect the rest of us becomes drastically muted.

The student activists from Marjory Stoneman Douglas High School did not waste their time trying to get the NRA's enablers to admit that the NRA was lying. Instead, they made it inconvenient for the NRA's enablers to continue to back the NRA. The power of the liar is diffused when their enablers fade away—which is exactly what the NRA found as a result of the student activists' actions.

Just a few weeks after the 2018 midterm elections, the NRA's financial filings revealed that they had lost $55 million in revenue in the past year. "The NRA took in more than $128 million in dues last year—a significant sum, but down considerably from the $163 million it took in the year prior."[7]

Insanity Trap #4:
Trying to Point Out Hypocrisy to the
Liar's Coattail Riders

As Matshona Dhliwayo observes, "When dealing with two-faced people, it is difficult to know which face is uglier, the real one or the manufactured one." A liar's coattail riders know that they are being hypocritical, but they don't care. Because they don't care, expending energy to prove the hypocrisy increases your probability of losing your mind without changing the unlikelihood that you will change their minds.

Since most of us are not habitual liars, we try to do our best to live our lives according to what we say we believe and value. Our efforts to be consistent in this way impel us to call out hypocrisy as disqualifying in some way. If a person says one thing but does another, we call out the hypocrisy as a way to discount what he is saying. But pointing out hypocrisy to a liar's coattail riders is an insanity trap. That's because reacting to hypocrisy is an emotional reaction, not a rational choice.

Hypocrisy reeks of insincerity, but the type and amount of energy it takes to focus on the hypocrisy and the hypocrites drains us way before hypocrites might even begin to care about what we think. Reacting to hypocrisy relies on emotional reflexes that are triggered when there is incongruence in what people say in light of what they do.

In many ways, this emotional reflex is connected to our survival instincts; someone who isn't a hypocrite feels safer and more reliable than someone who is a hypocrite. Once our survival instincts are activated, our reactions become more reflexive and less deliberate. As Scott Aikin and Robert Talisse wrote in an article published in *Scientific American*:

> To skirt this danger, people should suppress their instinctual responses to accusations of duplicity so that they can focus on the real issues at hand. Such concentration is essential to our ability to rationally judge our leaders, colleagues and friends

as well as to make decisions about important social issues that affect our lives.[8]

The strategy to avoid this insanity trap is to recognize that a liar's coattail riders do not care if they are hypocrites; they do care if their reputations and credibility are sullied by aligning themselves with the liar. Since coattail riders are in the game to leverage the liar's lies to their own benefit—without getting their own hands dirty in the process—using facts to tether the liar to the coattail riders as the liar continues to defend himself forces the coattail riders to distance themselves and revoke the cover they provide to the liars. It's a strategy similar to the neutralization of enablers, but it has to be subtler in its execution because coattail riders cannot allow themselves to be as directly tied to the liars as the enablers are.

Bill O'Reilly's Coattails

Bill O'Reilly started at Fox News in 1996 when the cable news outlet was just a fledgling start-up. By 2001, "The O'Reilly Factor became the country's most watched cable news program,"[9] and the show went on to dominate nightly cable news for almost two decades. Known for his blunt and often controversial commentary and interviewing style, O'Reilly's ability to attract almost a million viewers every night led to the show earning "$446 million from advertisers between 2014 and 2016."[10]

But, O'Reilly's shining star sported an undercurrent of bad behavior that both O'Reilly and Fox News did their best to hide. In October 2004, *The Washington Post* reported that "Bill O'Reilly settled a sexual harassment lawsuit by his former producer" for millions of dollars.[11] And, in 2017:

> *The New York Times* reported that O'Reilly and Fox News have settled sexual harassment and verbal abuse claims with five different women aimed at the host over the years. The two settlements mentioned above had been previously reported, but three were unknown. The payouts to women to end their suits total $13 million.[12]

More women broke their silence and spoke up about how O'Reilly had harassed and abused them while they were working for Fox News. Throughout the steady exposure of his bad behavior, O'Reilly denied all allegations and accused the media (all media except Fox News) to be against him because he was so successful.

As continued media coverage of the settlements that O'Reilly and Fox News had executed to keep women silent exposed evidence that O'Reilly was clearly lying, Fox News continued to support him and tell the world that they believed him rather than the evidence that was piling up against him.

O'Reilly was a malignant liar, and Fox News was one of his staunchest enablers. In addition to his enablers, O'Reilly had another contingency of players who were making his survival and success possible—players who weren't directly involved in anything that happened at Fox News or on O'Reilly's show but benefitted from his success nonetheless: the show's sponsors.

O'Reilly's sponsors advertised on his show because it was a successful show that reached more than a million viewers every day. O'Reilly's sponsors were his coattail riders, leveraging the show's success for their benefit without having to get their hands dirty with any day-to-day business of the show and/or Fox News.

As sexual harassment victim advocates and other such advocacy groups readied themselves to fight and win against Bill O'Reilly, they realized that they couldn't go after O'Reilly directly: Trying to prove that he was lying was futile because he had a bigger platform than they did. They also realized that they couldn't go after Fox News directly because Fox News had invested heavily in enabling him.

The advocates targeted the coattail riders—i.e., O'Reilly's sponsors—by asking them repeatedly on social media if they wanted to be associated with someone who settled so many sexual harassment suits. The advocates didn't accuse O'Reilly of lying; they picked a fact—i.e., he had settled lawsuits—and they used that fact to question the sponsors' support for O'Reilly's show.

On April 4, 2017, "O'Reilly sponsors began to jump ship. Eleven O'Reilly sponsors exited the show, including Mercedes-Benz, Hyundai, Mitsubishi,

BMW, GlaxoSmithKline, Allstate, T. Rowe Price and Constant Contact."[13] The next day, April 5, more advertisers announced they were leaving, including "Lexus, Credit Karma, Bayer, TrueCar, Wayfair, Orkin, Society for Human Resources Management, CFP Board and Coldwell Banker. The total number of sponsors departing the show now totaled at least 20."[14] By April 7, more than sixty sponsors had severed their relationships with O'Reilly's show. On April 19, Fox News announced that it had ended its relationship with Bill O'Reilly.

The sponsors acted in their best interests and decided that foregoing the opportunity to reach O'Reilly's audience was a better business decision than getting sullied through their association with him.

The hypocrisy of many of these sponsors did not go unnoticed by the sexual harassment victim advocates. They whispered among themselves about how these same sponsors had done nothing when, in 2006:

> O'Reilly referred to Jennifer Moore, an 18-year-old rape and murder victim, as "moronic" for getting her car towed in New York City while she was drunk. He also insinuated that her inebriation and manner of dress were at least partially to blame for her death: "She was 5-foot-2, 105 pounds, wearing a miniskirt and a halter top with a bare midriff. Now, again, there you go. So every predator in the world is gonna pick that up at two in the morning."[15]

> The same sponsors also had stuck with O'Reilly after he: equated the use of birth control with sexual activity, asking Sandra Fluke, a Georgetown law student who testified before Congress regarding mandated insurance coverage of contraceptives, "You want me to give you my hard-earned money so you can have sex?" He went on to say that Sandra Fluke "clearly wanted society to pay for her activities," and equated the government mandating contraceptive coverage to the government purchasing football equipment for college football teams.[16]

Bill O'Reilly had never tried to hide who he was or what he believed—especially about women—but the same sponsors who decided in 2017 that O'Reilly's show's values didn't align with their corporate values previously had never noticed or cared about this misalignment.

Hypocrisy duly noted, but the hypocrisy was irrelevant. The goal was to decrease the coattail riders so that the liar and his enablers were more isolated. Once the coattail riders abandoned ship, Fox News decided that it was no longer in its best interest to be O'Reilly's enabler.

The sexual harassment advocates won against O'Reilly … without losing their minds.

Insanity Trap #5: Trying to Shame Liars

Shame is reserved for those who care about doing the right thing. Shame is for those who generally are anchored to facts and stray from them every once in a while. Malignant liars are not anchored to the truth, so there is no way to shame them. There are ways to take them down, but shaming them isn't one of them.

The best strategy to not fall into this insanity trap is to make peace with the fact that liars probably will never admit that they are lying. Liars—and especially malignant liars—will lie with their last breath. Liars will never take responsibility for their lying. Outsmarting them depends on preventing their lies from impacting your life, not on preventing them from lying or on shaming them into admitting the lies.

> As one journalist noted about Donald Trump and his lying: If you are operating from the premise that if you catch Trump red-handed in some lie he will have to confess and apologize, you will be disappointed every time. When Trump's explanation for firing FBI director James Comey contradicted that of his spokespeople, the deceit could not have been more obvious. Reporters dutifully pointed this out, no doubt expecting

the kind of contrition or clarification displayed by previous presidents. None came.

Similarly, when Trump suggested that former adviser Carter Page would "blow away" all allegations of his administration's collaboration with Russian agents provocateurs, the press noted that Trump had denied ever speaking to Page just a few months ago. Surely Trump had to own up to some deceit here, was the implicit tone of the reporting. And again, the implicit response from Trump was, No, I don't.

Trump ignored these attempts to shame him for falsehoods, just as he ignored all the fact-checking during the campaign. Why should Trump care about the truth when he can just continue what he's doing? It's worked so far.[17]

Making peace with the fact that a liar will probably never admit that he or she is lying doesn't mean that you give up the fight. It means that you realize that you won't win against malignant liars if you lose your mind trying to get them to do things they will never do.

Chapter 8:
Know Your Game, Define Your Win, and Identify Your Team

Self-esteem is reliance on one's power to think. It cannot be replaced by one's power to deceive. The self-confidence of a scientist and the self-confidence of a con man are not interchangeable states, and do not come from the same psychological universe. The success of a man who deals with reality augments his self-confidence. The success of a con man augments his panic.
—Ayn Rand

It's important to remember and acknowledge that it's human nature to want to correct "incorrect information" or "falsehoods" or "alternative facts" coming from any source. Our instinct to correct others based on what we know is deeply connected to our survival instinct and our communal nature. If other people—especially people who we are connected to in any way—are misinformed, that can mean danger for us. Recognizing and acknowledging this instinct allows us to understand our corrections of others.

It is equally important to step back after the correction and carefully notice how the person we corrected is engaging with the contradictory information. Are they engaging in listening behaviors such as leaning forward, nodding their heads up and down, and asking questions? Or are they engaging in ignoring behaviors such as leaning back, shaking their heads from side to side, crossing their arms, and interrupting to get their point heard?

If someone is engaging in listening behaviors, the errors in their information can be interpreted as them being mistaken or incorrect. When we believe that we could be mistaken, we are more likely to listen to information that will allow us to correct ourselves. However, if someone is engaged in ignoring behaviors, it is safe to assume either that they are not open to changing their beliefs, which are usually based on lies, or that they know they are misstating the facts (i.e., lying) and they aren't going to give up their lies. In either scenario, once you see that someone is responding to you with ignoring behaviors, do not waste your breath with any more words. And, once you stop trying to convince liars and believers of liars, you can start outsmarting them.

Since the probability of beating liars at their game is infinitely small, you have to know what game you want to play instead, define what winning looks like for you, and identify the various people who can be on your team. One of the primary reasons that people get caught in malignant liars' games is that there isn't a clear alternative that they can articulate for themselves to extricate themselves from the fake worlds crafted by malignant liars.

Know Your Game

If we take a closer look at the lies that initially made Enron successful and the facts that finally brought Enron down, we can see that Sherron Watkins, the Enron executive who blew the whistle on Enron's fraudulent account practices, recognized the game that Kenneth Lay, Jeffrey Skilling, and Andrew Fastow were playing. She didn't want to play that game.

The game Watkins wanted to play was that of taking effective fiduciary and strategic care of the company for which she worked. In playing this game, she sent an anonymous memo to Lay expressing her concerns.

When she saw that nothing was changing, she wrote Lay another memo that revealed who she was and why she was concerned. Nothing changed. She met with him and told him that she was concerned about the sustainability and reputation of the company. She did not go outside the company with her information, but when her memos to Lay were leaked to Congressional investigators, she agreed to testify regarding everything she knew. In an interview after the Congressional hearings, Watkins said:

> I do believe that executives rationalize their pay packages as well as aggressive accounting and other problem areas. My biggest concern for corporate America right now is that we have so few truly ethical leaders. The Enron scandal was the first, followed by a whole slew of others, and we discovered with each scandal that the watchdog groups that are in business to protect investors failed: auditors, outside lawyers, Wall Street research analysts, and the nation's largest banks. After all the corporate scandals, we had the Wall Street scandals—tainted stock research, among other things. Then the mutual fund scandal with money managers trading against their own customers for personal gain, trading after hours, and giving preferential treatment to larger customers. Next we had the insurance industry scandal unearthed by Elliot Spitzer. Now it's outsized CEO pay packages and option backdating.
>
> In order to flourish, a successful capitalist system—really any system, be it education, medicine, business, or government—must be predicated on fairness, honesty, and integrity. In fact, many scholars describe the capitalist system as a three-legged stool—one based on economic freedom, political freedom, and moral responsibility. A weakness in any one leg and the stool topples.[18]

Liars lie to get what they want. They are not tethered to facts or ethics or anything else that the majority of us depend on in order to trust each other and the institutions that are our governments, our workplaces, and our communities. The liars whom Watkins was dealing with were playing the game of getting the most money and power they could, regardless of what they were doing to the company, its employees, and its investors.

Playing their game would have meant trying to out them as liars, which would have exhausted and destroyed anyone without the resources that Lay, Skilling, and Fastow collectively had. Watkins played a different game. She didn't call them liars; she called them ineffective at the job of caring for the company and its various constituents, and she did it because she cared about the company and about doing the right thing.

Define Your Win

When interacting with a malignant liar, winning cannot be focused on either getting the liar to back down or proving the liar is lying. Liars will not back down. They are working to get away with lying as opposed to creating a reputation as a truth teller. Any effort poured into thwarting either of these two goals will be not only ineffective and fruitless but exhausting and frustrating to anyone to tries.

So, what does winning look like for you? You have to decide—based on the game you have decided to play—what positive outcomes you desire. Once you identify these outcomes, you have to keep these outcomes at the forefront of your thinking in order to navigate interactions with liars.

Deep Throat

"You do not need to defeat a liar, a liar's lie is itself his or her defeat."
—Ehsan Sehgal

In 1972, a secret government informant gave Bob Woodward, a reporter at *The Washington Post*, crucial information that personally linked President Richard Nixon to the Watergate scandal. Dubbed "Deep Throat" by Howard Simmons, the managing editor of *The Washington Post* during that time, this secret informant's information was one of the key triggers to the untenability of Nixon continuing to lie.

Nixon was lying to the people of the United States, and he was lying to cover up his lies in order to stay in power. Nixon's believers and enablers were pushing the lies every chance they got. His coattail riders also were working to keep the lies afloat so that they, too, could continue to benefit from his presidency.

Deep Throat outsmarted Nixon by covertly providing the *Post* the information they needed to publicly debunk Nixon's lies. The public did not discover his identity as Mark Felt until 2005, more than thirty years after he began covertly communicating with Woodward.

Felt defined his winning as taking Nixon down and getting him out of office. If Felt had defined winning as getting Nixon to publicly admit that he was lying, not only would he have lost that battle, but he might not have won the battle of getting him out of office, either.

Since most of us live our lives within a framework of honesty and fairness, the unfairness of a malignant liar's wins can haunt us. But we must not get pulled into the emotional chaos of chasing justice because liars thrive on that chaos. As the saying goes, never wrestle with a pig because both of you will get dirty, but the pig will actually enjoy it. When battling liars, we have to avoid defining wins in the context of the liar facing any type of justice and pragmatically define what we want for ourselves.

Identify Your Team

Once you know the game you want to play and define what winning looks like for you, take a moment to reflect on who might want the same positive outcomes that you do. These are people who can be on your team even if you have nothing else in common than the desire to achieve the positive outcomes you are seeking to achieve.

The liars have believers of lies, enablers of liars, and coattail riders, but people seeking to outsmart liars also have people on our side: We have believers of facts, supporters of fairness and justice, and people who do the right thing. We might not always know who they are, but once we show up to play our game, they will show up to play alongside us. What's more is that we don't have to know who the individuals are, but we can identify the types of people who can be on our team so that we know we won't always be alone in these fights.

Bill Cosby

A storyteller makes up things to help other people; a liar makes up things to help himself.
—Daniel Wallace

Bill Cosby was a comedian, actor, writer, director, producer, and game show host—and one of the most entertaining storytellers of his time. He lived the lavish life of a wealthy celebrity. Bill Cosby is now (and will be for the next three to ten years) Inmate NN7687 at SCI Phoenix, a maximum-security state prison in Pennsylvania.

Cosby's precipitous fall from "America's Dad" to Inmate NN7687 can be credited to Andrea Constand, the former director of operations for Temple University's women's basketball team.

In early 2004, Constand visited Cosby at his home in Cheltenham Township in Montgomery, Pennsylvania, to seek career advice from one of Temple University's most famous and influential boosters. During her visit, Cosby gave her a couple of pink pills that he said would help relax her. Then he sexually assaulted her. The drugs Cosby had given Constand disabled her ability to move or speak. In March 2004, Constand resigned from Temple University and returned home to Ontario, Canada. She told no one about the sexual assault.

One year later, Constand woke up one morning from a flashback-induced nightmare about her assault, and she told her mother about it. As she and her mother talked, Constand reviewed the pros and cons of her alternative courses of action, and she realized that, beyond the damage she felt she received at Cosby's hands, she was frightened for other women whom he could and would hurt. Constand reported her assault.

She was very clear about the game she wanted to play and why: She wanted to speak out about her assault and make sure that there was enough information about who Cosby was in order to prevent other women from trusting him. For her, the win was shining public attention on Cosby and his misdeeds. She didn't really think that people would believe her, and she feared that Cosby would not pay the price in any significant way.

Her fear was soon confirmed after her complaint was filed. Cosby denied all the charges, and Montgomery County District Attorney Bruce Castor decided not to proceed with the case because of a lack of credible and sufficient evidence. Cheltenham Police Chief John Norris told *Vanity Fair* that Cosby "came in wearing the typical Cosby sweater … [he] was a gentleman. I don't think he was evasive … he said it was a consensual sexual encounter." Cosby lied to the police chief, and the police chief believed him. He conveyed that belief to Castor, who decided that, based on what Cosby had said, there was insufficient evidence to move forward.

But Andrea Constand had already won the game she had been playing. The media attention to her complaint and Castor's decision to not prosecute resulted in more than a dozen additional women coming forward with stories about how they, too, were assaulted by Cosby, going back to the late 1960s. More people had emerged to be Constand's teammates in the game she chose to play. In March 2005, Constand filed a civil law suit against Cosby that included sworn depositions from thirteen additional women who said that Cosby had sexually victimized them. Cosby settled for more than $3 million.

Constand's efforts continued to bear fruit even after the settlement was reached. More women came out publicly. Cosby stepped down from Temple University's Board of Trustees. His honorary degrees were revoked. In December 2015, Cosby was charged with criminally drugging and sexually assaulting Constand. Two years later, in June 2017, Cosby's trial ended in a mistrial. The prosecutor announced that he would retry the case.

Finally, on April 26, 2018, Cosby was convicted on three counts of aggravated indecent assault. On September 25, 2018, Cosby was sentenced to three to ten years in prison.

Cosby had lied until the day of his sentencing, and he continues to lie. Expecting Cosby to tell the truth is an exercise in extreme futility, but we don't need liars to tell the truth to outsmart them. We just need to keep our eyes on the game we want to play and on what winning actually means to us.

Liars have their believers, enablers, and coattail riders on their teams. But each of us can create a team when we go up against liars: There are believers, supporters, and do-the-right-thingers who are waiting to be on our teams as soon as we make room for them to do so.

The Ten-Question Game Plan to Win Against Liars

Although it sounds simple enough to ask you to know the game you want to play, define what winning looks like for you, and identify the people who can be on your team, the process can be difficult start. The following questions can help you get started:

1. Who is the liar, and how is the liar connected to you?

2. What are the lies the liar tells?

3. Why do you think the person is lying? (It's useful here to try to identify which of the usual fears the liar is trying to avoid: fear of losing, fear of not having control, fear of not fitting in, fear of rejection, fear of embarrassment, fear of boredom, fear of anxiety, and/ or fear of confrontation or punishment)

4. How do the lies affect you?

5. If the lies didn't exist, what could you do that you can't do right now? What are the lies preventing you from doing?

6. Who can be on your team?

7. Who is on the liar's team? Who are the liar's believers, enablers, and coattail riders?

8. What are all the ways in which you can play to win against this liar?

9. What are the costs and benefits of the different wins you can pursue?

10. Which win makes the most sense to pursue?

We applied these questions at my firm in dealing with a potential client who turned out to not be a potential client at all. Let's take a look at how this can work.

Believe Me: Using the Ten-Question Game Plan

Carla, a leadership development manager at a large firm, had contacted Nextions a couple of years ago and told us that her firm was looking to engage leadership development consultants, and we were her first choice. She asked us to put together a proposal, and she asked us for several calls during which she requested extensive details, numerous examples, and sample work product. We were used to potential clients needing more information after a proposal was submitted, but Carla's requests felt particularly onerous.

After our fourth pitch call with her, my team and I discussed how it felt like she was just trying to get work from us without paying for it. We pushed back when she requested another call, and she responded with, "Believe me, if it was up to me, I would have hired you already. The person who is making the decision on this is just one of those people who needs a lot of information before he can make a decision."

We gave her the benefit of the doubt and asked if it made sense for us to speak to the decisionmaker directly. She quickly said no and told us that he didn't like to deal directly with vendors. She followed up by saying again, "Believe me, I would never do this to you if I didn't have to."

We gently told her that we really felt she had all the information we could give without being formally engaged. She thanked us for our time—and never got back in touch with us.

Until a year later.

Carla contacted us and apologized that nothing had materialized the previous year. She explained that they had a new procurement system, a new vendor selection process, and said, "Believe me, it won't be like it was last year."

We gave her the benefit of the doubt again, and we figured that she wouldn't need the same amount of calls and information as the previous year since the answers would not be that different. We were wrong.

During our first pitch call in this round of communications, she told us that they were interested in hiring us to do a deeper level of leadership training. "Let's say we did everything we talked about doing last year," she said. "What would be the next level of work that you all can do for us?" We told her that the deeper level of work would require seeing the data from the previous work, understanding the impacts from the previous work, etc. We told her that it would be a tricky question to answer when we didn't actually do the work. She asked if we could respond to hypotheticals that she threw out. She said that they were interested in hiring consultants for a long-term engagement and needed to know what our capabilities were for beyond the initial work.

The pitch process didn't feel right to us, and we, again, gently told her that we felt that we should be engaged in some way in order to continue the conversation. Her response sounded familiar: "Believe me, I know how much we are asking of you, and I would have hired you a long time ago if it were up to me."

My team and I got together to discuss our next steps. One of my teammates pointed out how often Carla said "believe me" before she answered our questions. We paid attention to the red flag and decided to do some due diligence on her firm and on Carla herself.

We discovered that the firm had released several press releases over the past year about the work they would be doing in this year. Even a superficial read of the press releases told us how much the work they had done had mirrored the proposal we had provided. We called Carla and asked her about the press releases. Her response: "Believe me, I know how it looks. We weren't able to hire anyone last year, so I put some general stuff in place based on what we had discussed. Believe me, I know it's not anywhere near what you all would have been able to do for us."

Believe me, we understood.

It had not escaped our attention that Carla had been promoted from a manager to a director in the past year. It also had not escaped our attention that the new pitch cycle smelled a lot like the next level of ideas she needed to steal.

We used our Ten-Question Game Plan to help us understand how best to deal with Carla.

1. Who is the liar, and how is the liar connected to you?

   Our liar was Carla, and she was a potential client. She also knew a lot of people who worked for current clients and potential future clients.

2. What are the lies the liar tells?

   Carla was lying about the fact that she was seeking information as part of a process to hire a consulting firm. She was lying to get information that she was passing off as her own ideas and work product within her organization.

3. Why do you think the person is lying?

   Carla was lying because she was probably afraid of losing, not having control at work, not fitting, getting rejected for not knowing her job well, being embarrassed, and being confronted at work about wrongdoing.

4. How do the lies affect you?

   Carla's lies were wasting our time, putting our intellectual property at risk, and generally pissing us off.

5. If the lies didn't exist, what could you do that you can't do right now? What are the lies preventing you from doing?

   If we didn't have to deal with Carla and her lies, we could use the time we were wasting toward real pitches that could result in business, and we could be more peaceful and less pissed off.

6. Who can be on your team?

   There are possibly other consultants that Carla had done this to who could be on our team as well as people in Carla's organization who were under the impression that Carla was capable of doing the work that she was passing off as her own.

7. Who is on the liar's team? Who are the liar's believers, enablers, and coattail riders?

   We figured that the people with whom Carla worked and the people to whom she reported were her believers. We thought about the fact that some of them likely were enablers who knew she wasn't doing the work but didn't care because the work was getting done.

8. What are all the ways in which you can play to win against this liar?

   We can confront her. We can refuse to take her calls. We can try to find someone else at the organization to talk to. We can try to find other consultants that she's done this to. We can insist that we only talk with her if she included other people from her organization on the call.

9. What are the costs and benefits of the different wins you can pursue?

   Confronting her would feel good, but there would be no next step if she denied it, and that could give her material to disparage us in the marketplace. The same would be true if we stopped taking her calls. Finding other people in the organization and/or consultants would take too much time. Insisting (in a nice way) that she include other people from her organization would help both in terms of not taking up so much of our time and not giving her material to disparage us.

10. Which win makes the most sense to pursue?

    Insisting that she include other people form her organization on future pitch calls.

After conducting this analysis using the Ten-Question Game Plan, we told her that we would be happy to continue the conversation if she also invited others from her firm to join the conversation so that we could be more efficient.

We never heard from her again.

Margaret: Using the Ten-Question Game Plan

Margaret knew that Rick, the senior vice president to whom she reported, lied a lot, but she generally had been able to negotiate it by staying away from him as much as necessary and dealing with him only when she absolutely needed to. That changed when Margaret was promoted to vice president and her new responsibilities involved working more closely with Rick.

When I first met with Margaret, she already had done a lot of reflection on Rick's lies, examining why she thought he lied and the potential effects of his lies on her. We applied the Ten-Question Game Plan to help her organize her thoughts and create a plan of action:

1. Who is the liar, and how is the liar connected to you?

    Rick is the SVP that I report to directly.

2. What are the lies the liar tells?

- *claiming to forget conversations in which he made me any promises of new opportunities,*

- *trivializing concerns that I had raised as "hysterical" and "paranoid" even though I had been extremely calm in the conversations and offered substantive evidence for my concerns,*

- *claiming that company policies on leave and flexibility were discretionary (they weren't) and missing meetings that I set up with Human Resources to review the policies by claiming that he thought he had been invited to these meetings erroneously, and*

- *being falsely complimentary about me to the executive vice president that he reported to and making it harder for me to lodge complaints against him without sounding crazy.*

3. Why do you think the person is lying?

   I think he is afraid of losing, of losing control, of rejection/not being good enough, and of embarrassment that I may have more talent than him.

4. How do the lies affect you?

   Right now, they are driving me insane and keeping me from taking the full leave I deserve to take. I think the future impact will be that he will prevent me from getting promoted and negatively affect my career.

5. If the lies didn't exist, what could you do that you can't do right now? What are the lies preventing you from doing?

   I would be able to the take the full leave I need—I want to travel somewhere and unplug! I also could create a career development plan based on what I want to achieve instead of how to get around Rick.

6. Who can be on your team?

   Other senior executives, maybe other people who report to him or have reported to him in the past, and my assistant.

7. Who is on the liar's team? Who are the liar's believers, enablers, and coattail riders?

   I think Rick's peers and many of the people who report up to him believe many of his lies. The people that Rick reported to, I just can't believe that everyone believes him. I think there may be some enablers there.

8. What are all the ways in which you can play to win against this liar?

   Complaining against him, confronting him directly, taking my leave regardless of what he says and seeing if he dings me, shake off his ability to affect me emotionally.

9. What are the costs and benefits of the different wins you can pursue?

   I don't think it will help my career if I complain against him or confront him. That will make me look weak and probably just make him gun even harder for me. I could take the leave, but I don't want to get dinged. I can maybe do something to distance myself from the stuff he does.

10. Which win makes the most sense to pursue?

Distancing myself in a way that protects me.

As we explored Margaret's answers, she could see how Rick lied in a way that made her constantly wonder if she actually remembered what she thought she remembered and if she actually was going crazy.

We created a plan that would allow Margaret to distance herself emotionally from Rick's lies but still give her the peace of mind that she was protecting herself if he got agitated and retaliated when he realized he wasn't getting a reaction from her. The list included Margaret:

- writing down everything in their conversations and emailing him the notes afterward to confirm what they had discussed, ending the email with a direct request to correct anything that he saw as inaccurate;

- sending him a separate email with specific action items for herself and for him with due dates and again asking him to correct anything that he saw as inaccurate;

- copying others on emails as much as possible when she could, and if it felt inappropriate to copy teammates, to at least copy her executive assistant;

- having conversations with others present as much as possible, such as asking him a question at the end of a meeting so that others were around; and

- identifying one or two people whom she trusted and to whom she spoke to regularly about what was going on with Rick and discussing her strategies to deal with his lies, and

- finding ways to get in front of other executives so that they could get their own impressions of her.

Two months later, Margaret's strategies were working in decreasing Rick's lies, but she did notice that he was angrier and more withdrawn around her. She initially felt drained after seeing him, but she started feeling more in control over his ability to unfairly affect her career, which allowed her to get less and less drained. She had heard from others that he spoke negatively about her when she wasn't around, but she knew that his own lies about her in the past would protect her from him going too far.

She told me that she realized that she was winning against Rick even if winning took a lot of work and was exhausting. She lamented that it would just feel so much better to work with someone who was not a malignant liar, but recognized that her ability to get around Rick was giving her insights into liars, herself, and people in general. She decided to see these insights as lessons that would help her far beyond her interactions with Rick.

Evelyn: Using the Ten-Question Game Plan

Evelyn was a junior executive in a highly competitive firm, and although she loved her work and her colleagues, she was getting nervous about her prospects for advancement because of her interactions with Adam, the person who would be responsible for putting her name up for promotion and advocating for her.

Within just a few months of working for Adam, Evelyn realized that he treated her differently than her peers (who were all men). She also noticed that he often lied to her in direct and indirect ways.

On one project, for example, he gave her directions on whom should staff a particular project. Then, in front of their full team, he chided her for staffing the project that way: "Why didn't you just do what I asked you to? Why do I bother helping you and giving you directions as to what you should do when you don't follow directions?" When she went to his office after the meeting to figure out why he had berated her for doing exactly what he had asked her to do, he told her that she must have misunderstood what he had initially told her. He also told her that he had not yelled at her and that she was being too sensitive.

On a different project, he sent her the wrong address for a client meeting. When Evelyn realized that she was not in the right place, she contacted Adam's assistant and got the right address. She made it to the client meeting just a few minutes before the meeting started, and Adam introduced her to the client as the "perpetually late Evelyn." When it was her turn to present in the meeting, he asked one of her male colleagues to do the presentation instead. When she asked him after the meeting why he had taken the opportunity away from her, he told her that she was misreading the situation and he was actually being compassionate because he figured that she was stressed out from being late.

Soon thereafter, Adam took to calling Evelyn "Evie" and insisted on doing so even when she told him that she preferred Evelyn. He told her that he preferred "Evie" because it took less time to say.

Evelyn was one of the first people who agreed to put the research in this book to use, and we started working together in creating a game plan for a win. We started with the Ten-Question Game Plan.

1. Who is the liar, and how is the liar connected to you?

   Liar is Adam. He is one of the people I report to and he can make or break my next promotion.

2. What are the lies the liar tells?

   It's almost like he tells lies to make me fail. If I have the right information, I work hard and do really good work. If someone lies to me, I don't get the information I need to succeed.

3. Why do you think the person is lying?

   Adam is definitely scared of not having control, and I think he is anxious about being around a successful woman. I think this anxiety is what made him give me that ridiculous nickname.

4. How do the lies affect you?

   They threaten my ability to advance.

5. If the lies didn't exist, what could you do that you can't do right now? What are the lies preventing you from doing?

   I could be focused on doing projects where I grow instead of running around undoing the stupid stuff that Adam does.

6. Who can be on your team?

   Peers, maybe female executives, maybe other men in the company, and definitely Adam's assistant.

7. Who is on the liar's team? Who are the liar's believers, enablers, and coattail riders?

   I think the top people believe him, but I'm not sure they enable him.

8. What are all the ways in which you can play to win against this liar?

   I'm too competitive to play to not lose. I want to win. I know you said that I can't be stubborn about seeing him brought down a notch or two, but that can be an indirect goal, right?

9. What are the costs and benefits of the different wins you can pursue?

   If I'm too direct, I'll be labeled a bitch. If I confront him, he will just deny it. He will make it a joke and make me look like I'm a bad sport. I have to be more subtle. I think I like the idea of building my team.

10. Which win makes the most sense to pursue?

   Build my team so that I'm not fighting his crazy alone.

Evelyn first worked to make sure that she wasn't second-guessing herself on the facts given the lying that Adam was doing. She realized that she had spent a lot of time focused on proving that Adam was lying instead of thinking about what she wanted and why his lying was preventing her from getting what she wanted. She wanted to get promoted, and she feared that Adam's lies were creating a narrative in which she not only would not get promoted but actually might get fired.

When she started thinking about who was on her team, Evelyn realized that she had not actively tried to create a network for herself through which she could gather information, brainstorm strategies, and lean on other people. She identified a couple of her peers, a female executive who was Adam's peer but in a different part of the firm, and a woman who used to work on their team who had left for another firm. She sat down with each of the four people and explained what had been going on. She took their comments and insights into account while she considered what Adam's game could be, how he was trying to get away with lying, and who he relied upon in to win whatever game he was playing.

She learned from the female executive that there had been a couple of sexual discrimination complaints filed against Adam, and he was under a lot of pressure to demonstrate that he was fair and inclusive of women. She learned from talking with her peers that Adam had done similar things to some of the other men on the team as well. She learned from the woman who had left the firm that Adam's strategy for success had always been to blame the people who reported up to him for incompetency as a way to explain any negative outcomes for which he was responsible.

The conversations helped Evelyn realize that Adam wanted to advance in the firm without doing much work and that it was easier for him to lie and blame others than to do the work necessary to achieve real success.

Evelyn realized that she could not secure her position or the possibility for advancement if she was wholly dependent on Adam, so she volunteered to work on an ad hoc project with another executive. She also made a commitment to attend more of the firm's social events so that she could connect with people outside Adam's circle of influence. She befriended Adam's assistant so that she could get more accurate information on a regular basis. And, finally, she decided to make peace with Adam calling her Evie for a while until she had a broader and more solid base from which to fight back.

Evelyn also started to take better notes when Adam would give her directions or an assignment, and she began to confirm what he said by email before starting anything. As her network expanded, and as she became more confident in her ability to stand up to Adam, she realized that his lies didn't necessarily stop but that the impact of his lies on her life did decrease. She became closer with her peers, and they would step in if Adam completely misstated or misrepresented something that Evelyn had said or done. During one meeting, for example, Adam called her Evie, and one of her colleagues corrected him and told him that she really did prefer to be called Evelyn.

Evelyn and I talked several times as she deliberately navigated and eventually neutralized Adam's lies. With each conversation, I could hear how much confidence she was gaining in her ability to deal with Adam.

When I asked her who she thought Adam's believers, enablers, and coattail riders were, she told me that Adam's peers were his biggest believers and that the people to whom Adam reported were his enablers because they never asked tough questions or held him accountable for how he developed the people he managed. She wasn't sure who his coattail riders were, but knowing who his believers and enablers were had allowed her to more deliberately and successfully navigate her work environment and her network.

Conclusion:
Lessons From Now

The seeds of this book initially were sown soon after I wrote *One Size Never Fits All: Business Development Strategies Tailored for Women (and Most Men).* In researching gender differences in how men and women developed business differently in professional service firms and how they were recognized and rewarded differently for their efforts, I was surprised to find how often people (almost all men but a few women here and there as well) blatantly lied in their workplaces. The liars were not the slackers or underperformers; they were mostly powerful, successful men who lied when they made promises to others, lied when they took credit for others' work, lied when they abused their power and authority, and lied generally because they benefited from the lying. And they consistently got away with their lying.

In January 2016, I reached out to about twenty people to ask if they would be interested in talking with me about liars in their workplaces. I also asked them to see if there were others in their workplaces and/or networks who would be interested in speaking with me. By the end of April 2016, one hundred forty-three people from all different industries and types of workplaces wanted to talk to me about liars and lies in their workplaces.

The overwhelming number of people (82.5 percent) were women, and the majority of the men (72 percent) were men of color.

As I heard story after story, the presence of malignant liars in workplaces and the havoc they wreak began to emerge. By Summer 2016, I had gathered enough research to write a meaningful book on liars in the workplace. Then Donald J. Trump happened.

As the presidential campaign heated up in 2016, the subject of liars and lies was suddenly a hot topic for reporters, researchers, and millions of others who realized that the frameworks we had in place for assessing current and future leaders did not account for blatant and frequent lying.

News organizations started counting how many lies Trump told weekly. Researchers brushed off previous research to update it with current events. Psychologists provided psychological frameworks for organizing and understanding liars and lies. People everywhere were talking about lying in and out of their workplaces.

As mentioned in the Introduction, this book is about liars, the lies they tell, and how we can be smarter than those lies. This book is not a book about Trump or politics or the current state of discourse and dialogue in our country. But everything that has happened in our very recent past offers valuable lessons that reinforce the research on lying and highlights the power of effective strategies in a way that is useful to explore.

One Small Step for Facts, One Giant Leap for Truth

When powerful people lie, it can feel disempowering. But no matter how powerful people are, even the smallest of facts can start an avalanche that brings down even the most powerful of individuals and/or institutions. The downfall may not be immediate, but the smallest of facts can start the unraveling of lies in ways that make the lies unsustainable.

The leaders of Enron were considered brilliant businessmen until facts released by one woman made the leaders nothing more than lessons on how to never do business. Bill Cosby was considered an untouchable celebrity until one woman spoke her facts to power. The NRA was considered to be one of the most powerful kingmaking organizations in America until a few high school students decided to proliferate facts that have made the NRA impotent and brought it to the brink of bankruptcy. Trump was considered invincible until a steady drip of facts gave the opposing party an overwhelming victory in the 2018 midterm elections.

Facts are small but mighty things. Once you start shining a light on a lie with facts, the lie weakens and cannot ever return to full strength. The lie might not crumble immediately, but every fact puts a crack in the lie, and each new fact gains the necessary momentum to destroy the lie completely.

It's not easy to confront the liars and the lies they tell in our workplaces, but none of us is as powerless as we feel. We need to remember that part of a liar's game is to make us feel afraid, to doubt ourselves, and to refrain from taking action because we don't think we can do anything about the liars or their lies. We also need to remember that as soon as we reject fear and doubt, taking action with facts is not only possible but incredibly empowering, especially because facts give us the power to decide both which game we want to play and what winning means for us personally.

Win Without Losing Your Mind

Liars design their alternative worlds to make us feel like we are losing our minds, and winning against liars requires that we retain our sanity as we fight back with facts. The more we can learn about how liars lie, how lies work, why we believe lies, and how we can be smarter than the lies we encounter, the more equipped we will be to inoculate ourselves against the impact of the lies and stay sane in the process.

Sometimes, Just Laugh

When dealing with liars, sometimes you have to remember just to laugh at the ridiculousness of the lies they tell. When Trump first announced that he was running for president, *The Washington Post* very seriously started fact-checking his speeches using their Pinocchio scale: [1]

- One Pinocchio: Some shading of the facts. Selective telling of the truth. Some omissions and exaggerations, but no outright falsehoods. (You could view this as "mostly true.")

- Two Pinocchios: Significant omissions and/or exaggerations. Some factual error may be involved but not necessarily. A politician can create a false, misleading impression by playing with words and using legalistic language that means little to ordinary people. (Similar to "half true.")

- Three Pinocchios: Significant factual error and/or obvious contradictions. This gets into the realm of "mostly false." But it could include statements which are technically correct (such as based on official government data) but are so taken out of context as to be very misleading. The line between Two and Three can be bit fuzzy and we do not award half-Pinocchios. So we strive to explain the factors that tipped us toward a Three.

- Four Pinocchios: Whoppers.

By December 2018, Trump's lying and lies got so bad that *The Washington Post* created a new point on their Pinocchio scale: the Bottomless Pinocchio:

> The bar for the Bottomless Pinocchio is high: Claims must have received Three or Four Pinocchios from The Fact Checker, and they must have been repeated at least 20 times. Twenty is a sufficiently robust number that there can be no question the politician is aware that his or her facts are wrong. The list of Bottomless Pinocchios will be maintained on its own landing page. [2]

So far, the only person who has earned the Bottomless Pinocchio rating has been President Donald J. Trump.

Stopping, Not Finishing

Researching and writing this book in 2017 and 2018 was an adventure for which I was not adequately prepared. I often felt like the news was vomiting stories about liars and lying and lies at me at a rate I could barely take in. I wrote and rewrote sections of the book because the news cycle of the day presented an even better example of illustrating a particular point.

The conclusion was the hardest part of the book to write because I didn't know how to conclude when I feel like we are very much still in the middle of a conversation that we are dealing with every single day. So I decided that I am stopping at a certain point, but I'm not finished.

I thank each of you for engaging in this conversation with me, and I look forward to continuing the dialogue.

Endnotes

Introduction

1. Larry Kim, "17 Donald Trump Quotes That Are Surprisingly Brilliant," *Inc.*, August 24, 2015, https://www.inc.com/larry-kim/21-brilliant-quotes-from-the-donald-trump.html.

Section I: Understanding the Game

1. Daniel Wallace, *The Kings and Queens of Roam: A Novel*, (New York: Simon and Schuster, May 7, 2013).

2. Kim B. Serota and Timothy R. Levine, "A Few Prolific Liars: Variation in the Prevalence of Lying," *Journal of Language and Social Psychology* 34, no. 2 (2014), doi:10.1177/0261927x14528804.

3. Jesse Bering, "18 Attributes of Highly Effective Liars," *Scientific American*, July 7, 2011, https://blogs.scientificamerican.com/bering-in-mind/18-attributes-of-highly-effective-liars/.

4.   Bering, "18 Attributes."

5.   Jonathan Fields, "The Line Between Persuasion and Manipulation," *Jonathan Fields*, accessed March 11, 2019, http://www.jonathanfields.com/the-line-between-persuasion-and-manipulation/.

6.   Fields, "The Line."

7.   Brent Lang, "How New York Times Reporters Broke Hollywood's Biggest Sexual Harassment Story," *Variety*, accessed March 12, 2019, https://variety.com/2017/biz/features/new-york-times-harvey-weinstein-report-megan-twohey-jodi-kantor-1202637948/.

8.   Sara M. Moniuszko and Kara Kelly, "Harvey Weinstein Scandal: A Complete List of the 87 Accusers," *USA TODAY*, October 27, 2017, https://www.usatoday.com/story/life/people/2017/10/27/weinstein-scandal-complete-list-accusers/804663001/.

9.   Emily Smith, "Harvey Weinstein Gives First Interview After Shocking Sex Harassment Claims," *Page Six* October 5, 2017, https://pagesix.com/2017/10/05/harvey-weinstein-gives-first-interview-after-shocking-sex-harassment-claims/.

10. Kevin L. Kliesen, "The Economy Gets Back on Track: But Once Again Leaves Many Workers Behind," Federal Reserve Bank of St. Louis, last modified January 1, 2004, https://www.stlouisfed.org/publications/regional-economist/january-2004/the-economy-gets-back-on-track-but-once-again-leaves-many-workers-behind.

11. Divonne Smoyer, Kimberly Chow and Kelley Chittenden, "State Attorneys General Zero in on Elder Abuse, Health Services Industry Practices," *Lexology*, April 24, 2018, https://www.lexology.com/library/detail.aspx?g=0eaa29c5-400d-4d36-8963-8c489b90c200.

12. Clive Bates and Andy Rowell, *Tobacco Explained: The Truth About the Tobacco Industry…In Its Own Words*, (London: Action on Smoking and Health (ASH), n.d), http://www.who.int/tobacco/media/en/TobaccoExplained.pdf.

13. Peter Boyle et al., eds., *Tobacco: Science, Policy and Public Health* (New York, NY: Oxford University Press, 2010).

14. Tobacco Industry Research Committee, *A Frank Statement to Cigarette Smokers*, (New York, 1954), https://www.tobaccofreekids.org/assets/factsheets/0268.pdf.

15. Bates and Rowell, *Tobacco Explained.*

16. David Kessler, *A Question of Intent: A Great American Battle with a Deadly Industry* (New York, NY: PublicAffairs, 2002).

17. Chris Isidore, "Woman Who Sued Trump University Wants out of Case," *CNNMoney*, March 11, 2016, http://money.cnn.com/2016/03/11/news/companies/trump-university-donald-trump-tarla-makaeff/index.html.

18. Martin Samuels, Interview by Ira Flatow, "Scared to Death…Literally," *Talk of the Nation*, National Public Radio, October 26, 2012, https://www.npr.org/2012/10/26/163712863/scared-to-death-literally.

19. Etienne Benson, "The Synaptic Self," *Monitor on Psychology* 33, no. 10 (November 2002): 40, https://www.apa.org/monitor/nov02/synaptic.html.

20. "Mexicans in Mexico City Talk Trump, Hillary and Border Wall – But Not the One You're Thinking Of," *OC Weekly*, October 10, 2016, https://ocweekly.com/mexicans-in-mexico-city-talk-trump-hillary-and-border-wall-but-not-the-one-youre-thinking-of-7554688/.

21. Avi Selk, "'Rapist!' She Yelled at a Hispanic Man. 'She's Quoting the President,' He Thought," *The Washington Post*, June 26, 2018, https://www.washingtonpost.com/news/post-nation/wp/2018/06/26/rapist-she-yelled-at-a-hispanic-man-shes-quoting-the-president-he-thought/.

22. Sarah Gibbens, "Are We Born Fearing Spiders and Snakes?" *National Geographic*, October 26, 2017, https://news.nationalgeographic.com/2017/10/infant-fear-phobia-science-snakes-video-spd/.

23. Kendra Cherry, "What Was the Little Albert Experiment?" *Verywell Mind*, September 27, 2018, https://www.verywellmind.com/the-little-albert-experiment-2794994.

24. Julie Beck, "New Research Says There Are Only Four Emotions," *The Atlantic*, February 4, 2014, https://www.theatlantic.com/health/archive/2014/02/new-research-says-there-are-only-four-emotions/283560/.

25. Beck, "Four Emotions."

26. Chris Isidore, "Americans Spend More on the Lottery Than on …," *CNNMoney*, February 11, 2015, http://money.cnn.com/2015/02/11/news/companies/lottery-spending/.

27. Ronald L. Wasserstein, "A Statistician's View: What Are Your Chances of Winning the Powerball Lottery?" *HuffPost*, December 6, 2017, https://www.huffingtonpost.com/ronald-l-wasserstein/chances-of-winning-powerball-lottery_b_3288129.html.

28. Alvin Chang, "4 Ways the Lottery Preys on the Poor," *Vox*, January 13, 2016, https://www.vox.com/identities/2016/1/13/10763268/lottery-poor-prey.

29. Steve Tripoli, "Lotteries Take in Billions, Often Attract the Poor," *NPR*, July 16, 2014, https://www.npr.org/2014/07/16/332015825/lotteries-take-in-billions-often-attract-the-poor.

30. Derek Thompson, "Lotteries: America's $70 Billion Shame," *The Atlantic*, May 11, 2015, https://www.theatlantic.com/business/archive/2015/05/lotteries-americas-70-billion-shame/392870/.

31. Consumer Federation of America (CFA) and the Financial Planning Association (FPA), "How Americans View Personal Wealth vs. How Financial Planners View This Wealth," news release, January 9, 2006, Consumer Federation of America, https://consumerfed.org/pdfs/Financial_Planners_Study011006.pdf.

32. David Goldman, "Does Powerball Really Fund Education?" *CNNMoney*, January 14, 2016, http://money.cnn.com/2016/01/13/news/powerball-education/index.html.

33. Goldman, "Powerball."

34. "Where Does the Money Go: Good Causes," Illinois Lottery Official Site, accessed March 12, 2019, https://www.illinoislottery.com/giving-back/good-causes.

35. Fred Clark, "State Lotteries and Truth in Advertising," *Slacktivist*, November 14, 2014, https://www.patheos.com/blogs/slacktivist/2014/11/14/state-lotteries-and-truth-in-advertising/.

36. "Truth in Advertising and Marketing and Other FTC Regulations," HG.org, accessed March 12, 2019, https://www.hg.org/legal-articles/truth-in-advertising-and-marketing-and-other-ftc-regulations-31217.

37. Andrew Clott, "The Predatory Nature of State Lotteries," *Loyola Consumer Law Review* 28, no. 1 (2015), https://lawecommons.luc.edu/lclr/vol28/iss1/5/.

Section II:
Understanding the Opponent

1. Nicole Torres, "Most People Don't Want to Be Managers," *Harvard Business Review*, September 18, 2014, https://hbr.org/2014/09/most-people-dont-want-to-be-managers.

2. Nicole Torres, "Most People."

3. "Narcissistic Personality Disorder - Symptoms and Causes," *Mayo Clinic*, last modified November 18, 2017, https://www.mayoclinic.org/diseases-conditions/narcissistic-personality-disorder/symptoms-causes/syc-20366662.

4. Matthew Hutson, "Honest Liars: Dishonest Leaders May Be Perceived as Authentic," *Salon*, October 8, 2018, https://www.salon.com/2018/10/08/honest-liars-dishonest-leaders-may-be-perceived-as-authentic_partner/.

5. Greg Camp, "Rob Pincus Talks Storing Guns in a Child's Bedroom," *Guns.com*, June 18, 2016, https://www.guns.com/news/2016/06/18/rob-pincus-talks-storing-guns-in-childrens-bedrooms.

6. Robert McClendon, "5-year-old LaPlace Girl Dies After Shooting Herself with Handgun," *NOLA.com | The Times-Picayune*, May 21, 2016, https://www.nola.com/crime/2016/05/5-year-old_laplace_girl_dies_a.html.

7. Ryan Foley, Larry Fenn, and Nick Penzenstadler, "Chronicle of Agony: Gun Accidents Kill at Least 1 Kid Every Other Day," *USA TODAY*, October 14, 2016, https://www.usatoday.com/story/news/2016/10/14/ap-usa-today-gun-accidents-children/91906700/.

8. Kim Parker et al., "Guns in America: Attitudes and Experiences of Americans," *Pew Research Center*, June 22, 2017, http://www.pewsocialtrends.org/2017/06/22/americas-complex-relationship-with-guns/.

9. *Firearm Justifiable Homicides and Non-Fatal Self-Defense Gun Use: An Analysis of Federal Bureau of Investigation and National Crime Victimization Survey Data*, (Washington D.C.: Violence Policy Center, 2017), http://www.vpc.org/studies/justifiable17.pdf.

10. Katherine Ramsland, "Addicted to Lies: Reflex Fraud Explains the Enigma of Casey Anthony," *Psychology Today*, February 1, 2012, https://www.psychologytoday.com/us/blog/shadow-boxing/201202/addicted-lies.

11. Ramsland, "Addicted to Lies."

12. Ramsland, "Addicted to Lies."

13. Timothy R. Levine, Steven A. McCornak, and Hee S. Park, "Deception Research at Michigan State University," Michigan State University, accessed March 12, 2019, https://msu.edu/~levinet/deception.htm#Truth-Bias.

14. Jack Schafer, "Truth Bias: A Psychological Cloak for Deception," *Psychology Today*, June 26, 2013, https://www.psychologytoday.com/blog/let-their-words-do-the-talking/201306/truth-bias.

15. Linda Qiu, "Is Donald Trump's 'Art of the Deal' the Best-selling Business Book of All Time?" *PolitiFact*, July 6, 2015, http://www.politifact.com/truth-o-meter/statements/2015/jul/06/donald-trump/donald-trumps-art-deal-best-selling-business-book-/.

16. Alex Shephard, "Art of the Steal: How Trump Boosted His Book Sales and Gamed the New York Times Best-Seller List," *The New Republic*, September 18, 2017, https://newrepublic.com/article/144541/art-steal-trump-boosted-book-sales-gamed-new-york-times-best-seller-list.

17. Shephard, "Art of the Steal."

18. Harry G. Frankfurt, *On Bullshit,* (Princeton, NJ: Princeton University Press, 2009), 55-56.

19. Alana Abramson, "Trump Spoke About Everything from Puerto Rico to Robert Mueller," *Time*, October 16, 2017, http://time.com/4984507/donald-trump-mitch-mcconnell-rose-garden-press-conference/.

20. Etelka Lehoczky, "Spot a Liar," *Etelka Lehoczky*, 2005, https://www.etelkawrites.com/spot-a-liar.

21. Joe Navarro, "'Believe Me' What to Make of this Often-Used Phrase?" *Psychology Today*, August 31, 2017, https://www.psychologytoday.com/blog/spycatcher/201708/believe-me.

22. Maria Konnikova, "Trump's Lies Vs. Your Brain," *POLITICO Magazine*, January/February 2017, https://www.politico.com/magazine/story/2017/01/donald-trump-lies-liar-effect-brain-214658.

23. Konnikova, "Trump's Lies."

24. Konnikova, "Trump's Lies."

25. Harry McCracken, "Apple Adds an Asterisk to iPhone Ad," *Technologizer*, September 25, 2008, http://www.technologizer.com/2008/09/25/apple-adds-an-asterisk-to-iphone-ad/.

26. https://www.wired.com/images_blogs/gadgetlab/files/sc0081ad62.pdf

27. Tal Kopan, "Trump: 'We're Going to Destroy' MS-13," *CNN*, July 28, 2017, http://www.cnn.com/2017/07/28/politics/donald-trump-ms-13/index.html.

28. Sarah Sanders, Steven Mnuchin and H.R. McMaster, "Press Briefing by Press Secretary Sarah Sanders, Treasury Secretary Steven Mnuchin, and National Security Advisor H.R. McMaster." *The White House*, July 31, 2017, https://www.whitehouse.gov/briefings-statements/press-briefing-press-secretary-sarah-sanders-treasury-secretary-steven-mnuchin-national-security-advisor-h-r-mcmaster-073117/.

29. Jeff Stein, "Alabama Senate GOP Frontrunner: Constitution Was Written to 'Foster Christianity,'" *Vox*, September 26, 2017, https://www.vox.com/policy-and-politics/2017/9/26/16365774/judge-roy-moore-us-constitution.

30. Donald Trump, Marco Rubio, Ted Cruz, and Bernie Sanders, Interview by Chuck Todd, *Meet the Press*, NBC, February 21, 2016. https://www.nbcnews.com/meet-the-press/meet-press-february-21-2016-n523036.

31. Glenn Kessler and Michelle Ye Hee Lee, "Fact Checking Donald Trump's Presidential Announcement Speech," *The Washington Post*, June 17, 2015, https://www.washingtonpost.com/news/fact-checker/wp/2015/06/17/fact-checking-donald-trumps-presidential-announcement-speech/?utm_term=.723e8636b701.

32. Tom Kertscher, "Donald Trump's Racial Comments About Hispanic Judge in Trump University Case," *PolitiFact Wisconsin*, June 8, 2016, http://www.politifact.com/wisconsin/article/2016/jun/08/donald-trumps-racial-comments-about-judge-trump-un/.

33. Brent Kendall, "Trump Says Judge's Mexican Heritage Presents 'Absolute Conflict?'" *The Wall Street Journal*, June 3, 2016, https://www.wsj.com/articles/donald-trump-keeps-up-attacks-on-judge-gonzalo-curiel-1464911442.

34. Donald Trump, Interview by John Dickerson, *Face the Nation*, CBS, June 5, 2016, https://www.cbsnews.com/news/face-the-nation-transcripts-june-5-2016-trump/

35. Kertscher, "Donald Trump's Racial Comments."

36. "Hillary Clinton Mocks Donald Trump's 'Very Tall,' 'Beautiful' Wall," *The Week*, March 9, 2016, http://theweek.com/speedreads/611768/hillary-clinton-mocks-donald-trumps-tall-beautiful-wall.

37. Maggie Koerth-Baker, "Why Humans Are Bad at Spotting Lies," *FiveThirtyEight*, September 28, 2018, https://fivethirtyeight.com/features/why-humans-are-bad-at-spotting-lies/.

38. Nazneen Rahman, "Avoiding Confirmation Bias in Genetic Medicine," *The Transforming Genetic Medicine Initiative (TGMI)*, January 12, 2018, https://www.thetgmi.org/genetics/avoiding-confirmation-bias-genetic-medicine/.

39. Gilbert King, "The Smoothest Con Man That Ever Lived," *Smithsonian*, August 22, 2012, https://www.smithsonianmag.com/history/the-smoothest-con-man-that-ever-lived-29861908/.

40. "When Seeing IS Believing: Experts Find Loss of Control Leads People to Seek Order, Answers," *Kellogg School of Management, Northwestern University*, last modified October 2, 2008, https://www.kellogg.northwestern.edu/news_articles/2008/galinskyseeingisbelieving.aspx.

41. Pouya Entezami et al., "Historical Perspective on the Etiology of Rheumatoid Arthritis," *PubMed Central (PMC)*, February 1, 2012, https://www.ncbi.nlm.nih.gov/pmc/articles/PMC3119866/.

42. Steve Fishman, "Bernie Madoff, Free at Last," *New York Magazine*, June 6, 2010, http://nymag.com/news/crimelaw/66468/.

43. Molly Greenberg, "The Neuroscience of Motivation," *Kenan-Flagler Business School, University of North Carolina at Chapel Hill*, April 28, 2016, https://onlinemba.unc.edu/blog/neuroscience-motivation-kimberly-schaufenbuel/.

44. Tom Lutey, "Trump: 'We're Going to Win so Much, You're Going to be so Sick and Tired of Winning,'" *Billings Gazette*, May 26, 2016, https://billingsgazette.com/news/state-and-regional/govt-and-politics/trump-we-re-going-to-win-so-much-you-re/article_2f346f38-37e7-5711-ae07-d1fd000f4c38.html.

45. "We Are Biologically Programmed to Take Pleasure in the Pain of Those We Envy, Shows Study into Schadenfreude," *Daily Mail Online*, October 30, 2013, https://www.dailymail.co.uk/sciencetech/article-2479069/Schadenfreude-study-finds-likely-enjoy-misfortune-envy-them.html.

46. "Full Text: Donald Trump 2016 RNC Draft Speech Transcript," *POLITICO*, July 21, 2016, https://www.politico.com/story/2016/07/full-transcript-donald-trump-nomination-acceptance-speech-at-rnc-225974.

47. William P. Davis, "'Enemy of the People': Trump Breaks Out This Phrase During Moments of Peak Criticism." *The New York Times*, July 20, 2018, https://www.nytimes.com/2018/07/19/business/media/trump-media-enemy-of-the-people.html.

48. Graham Smith and Javier E. David, "Trump Launches Another Attack on the Media, Says Press Are 'Dangerous and Sick' and Can 'Cause War,'" *CNBC*, August 5, 2018, https://www.cnbc.com/2018/08/05/trump-steps-up-his-media-feud-saying-press-are-dangerous-and-sick.html.

49. Heather Timmons, "Watch: A Furious Tampa Crowd Screams at the Press, Just as Trump Intended," *Quartz*, August 1, 2018, https://qz.com/1345622/video-of-a-trump-rally-crowd-harassing-the-press-in-tampa/.

50. Douglas Ernst, "Jim Acosta Thanks Trump Supporter for Apology After Rally: 'We Had a Moment,'" *The Washington Times*, November 1, 2018, https://www.washingtontimes.com/news/2018/nov/1/jim-acosta-thanks-trump-supporter-for-apology-afte/.

51. Thomas B. Edsall, "Conservatives Vs. Liberals: More Than Politics," *HuffPost*, December 6, 2017, https://www.huffingtonpost.com/thomas-b-edsall/conservatives-vs-liberals_b_1262309.html.

52. "IN RE: Bernard L. Madoff Investment Securities LLC," *Findlaw*, Accessed March 13, 2019, https://caselaw.findlaw.com/us-2nd-circuit/1635547.html.

53. Lori Robertson, and Robert Farley, "The Facts on Crowd Size," *FactCheck.org*, January 24, 2017, http://www.factcheck.org/2017/01/the-facts-on-crowd-size/.

54. Sean Spicer, "Transcript of White House Press Secretary Statement to the Media," *POLITICO*, January 21, 2017, https://www.politico.com/story/2017/01/transcript-press-secretary-sean-spicer-media-233979.

55. Lori Robertson, and Robert Farley, "Facts on Crowd Size."

56. James Dator, "A Comprehensive Timeline of the Larry Nassar Case," *SBNation*, January 16, 2019, https://www.sbnation.com/2018/1/19/16900674/larry-nassar-abuse-timeline-usa-gymnastics-michigan-state.

57. Lesley Clark and David Lightman, "Evangelicals Slammed Bill Clinton's Sexual Misconduct. So Why Does Trump Get a Pass?" *McClatchyDC Bureau*, October 12, 2016, https://www.mcclatchydc.com/news/politics-government/election/article107819532.html.

58. Harriet Sherwood, "The Chosen One? The New Film That Claims Trump's Election Was an Act of God," *The Guardian*, October 3, 2018, https://www.theguardian.com/us-news/2018/oct/03/the-trump-prophecy-film-god-election-mark-taylor.

59. Ed Stetzer and Andrew MacDonald, "Why Evangelicals Voted Trump: Debunking the 81%," *Christianity Today*, October 18, 2018, https://www.christianitytoday.com/ct/2018/october/why-evangelicals-trump-vote-81-percent-2016-election.html.

60. Stetzer and MacDonald, "Debunking the 81%."

61. Sarah Jones, "Evangelicals Know Trump is a Liar. They Just Don't Care," *The New Republic*, June 8, 2017, https://newrepublic.com/minutes/143213/evangelicals-know-trump-liar-just-dont-care.

62. Jones, "Evangelicals."

Section III:
Winning Against Liars...
Without Losing Your Mind

1. Mark Molloy, "Donald Trump has Awkward Exchange with Reporter over False Election Claim," *The Telegraph*, February 18, 2017, https://www.telegraph.co.uk/news/2017/02/17/donald-trump-has-awkward-exchange-reporter-false-election-claim/.

2. Molloy, "Donald Trump has Awkward Exchange."

3. Molloy, "Donald Trump has Awkward Exchange."

4. Matthew Dessem, "Florida Shooting Survivor Emma Gonzalez to Trump: 'We Call BS,'" *Slate*, February 17, 2018, https://slate.com/news-and-politics/2018/02/florida-shooting-survivor-emma-gonzalez-to-trump-we-call-bs.html.

5. Philip Bump, "52 Senators Have an A-minus NRA Rating or Higher—Including Four Democrats," *The Washington Post*, February 15, 2018, https://www.washingtonpost.com/news/politics/wp/2018/02/15/52-senators-have-an-a-minus-nra-rating-or-higher-including-four-democrats/?utm_term=.f99139965516.

6. Aaron Kessler, "Why the NRA is so Powerful on Capitol Hill, by the Numbers," *CNN*, February 23, 2018, https://www.cnn.com/2018/02/23/politics/nra-political-money-clout/index.html.

7. Lachlan Markay, "The NRA Just Reported Losing $55 Million in Income," *The Daily Beast*, November 27, 2018, https://www.thedailybeast.com/the-nra-just-reported-losing-dollar55-million-in-income.

8. Scott F. Aikin and Robert B. Talisse, "The Truth about Hypocrisy," *Scientific American*, December 1, 2018, https://www.scientificamerican.com/article/the-truth-about-hypocrisy/.

9. Biography.com Editors, "Bill O'Reilly Biography," *The Biography.com website*, Last modified April 5, 2018, https://www.biography.com/people/bill-oreilly-9542547.

10. Phil Hornshaw, "Bill O'Reilly Sexual Harassment Scandal: Complete Timeline of Events (Photos)," *The Wrap*, April 19, 2017, https://www.thewrap.com/bill-oreilly-sexual-harassment-scandal-timeline/.

11. Howard Kurtz, "Bill O'Reilly, Producer Settle Harassment Suit," *The Washington Post*, October 29, 2004, http://www.washingtonpost.com/wp-dyn/articles/A7578-2004Oct28.html.

12. Hornshaw, "Bill O'Reilly."

13. Hornshaw, "Bill O'Reilly."

14. Hornshaw, "Bill O'Reilly."

15. Erin Nyren, "Bill O'Reilly's Most Shocking Quotes: The Hoodie, ACLU Terrorists and Victim-Blaming," *Variety*, April 19, 2017, https://variety.com/2017/tv/news/bill-oreilly-wildest-quotes-1202390457/.

16. Nyren, "Shocking Quotes."

17. Matthew Callan, "What My Father the Pathological Liar Taught Me About Trump," *VICE*, June 6, 2017, https://www.vice.com/en_us/article/7xpb8x/what-my-father-the-pathological-liar-taught-me-about-trump.

18. Dick Carozza, "Interview with Sherron Watkins: Constant Warning," *Fraud Magazine*, January/February 2007, http://www.fraud-magazine.com/article.aspx?id=583.

Conclusion:
Lessons From Now

1. Glenn Kessler, "About the Fact Checker," *The Washington Post*, January 1, 2017, https://www.washingtonpost.com/news/fact-checker/about-the-fact-checker/?utm_term=.1acdf5d02f8c.

2. Kessler, "About the Fact Checker."

Bibliography

Abramson, Alana. "Trump Spoke About Everything from Puerto Rico to Robert Mueller." *Time*. October 16, 2017. http://time.com/4984507/donald-trump-mitch-mcconnell-rose-garden-press-conference/.

Aikin, Scott F. and Robert B. Talisse. "The Truth about Hypocrisy." *Scientific American*. December 1, 2018. https://www.scientificamerican.com/article/the-truth-about-hypocrisy/.

Bates, Clive, and Andy Rowell. *Tobacco Explained: The Truth About the Tobacco Industry...In its Own Words*. London: Action on Smoking and Health (ASH), n.d. http://www.who.int/tobacco/media/en/TobaccoExplained.pdf.

Beck, Julie. "New Research Says There Are Only Four Emotions." *The Atlantic*. February 4, 2014. https://www.theatlantic.com/health/archive/2014/02/new-research-says-there-are-only-four-emotions/283560/.

Benson, Etienne. "The Synaptic Self." *Monitor on Psychology* 33, no. 10 (November 2002), 40. https://www.apa.org/monitor/nov02/synaptic.html.

Bering, Jesse. "18 Attributes of Highly Effective Liars." *Scientific American*. July 7, 2011. https://blogs.scientificamerican.com/bering-in-mind/18-attributes-of-highly-effective-liars/.

Biography.com Editors. "Bill O'Reilly Biography." *The Biography.com website.* Last modified April 5, 2018. https://www.biography.com/people/bill-oreilly-9542547.

Boyle, Peter, Nigel Gray, Jack Henningfield, Witold Zatonski, and John Seffrin, editors. *Tobacco: Science, Policy and Public Health*. New York, NY: Oxford University Press, 2010.

Bump, Philip. "52 Senators Have an A-minus NRA Rating or Higher— Including Four Democrats." *The Washington Post*. February 15, 2018. https://www.washingtonpost.com/news/politics/wp/2018/02/15/52-senators-have-an-a-minus-nra-rating-or-higher-including-four-democrats/?utm_term=.f99139965516.

Callan, Matthew. "What My Father the Pathological Liar Taught Me About Trump." *VICE*. June 6, 2017. https://www.vice.com/en_us/article/7xpb8x/what-my-father-the-pathological-liar-taught-me-about-trump.

Camp, Greg. "Rob Pincus Talks Storing Guns in a Child's Bedroom." *Guns.com*. June 18, 2016. https://www.guns.com/news/2016/06/18/rob-pincus-talks-storing-guns-in-childrens-bedrooms.

Carozza, Dick. "Interview with Sherron Watkins: Constant Warning." *Fraud Magazine*. January/February 2007. http://www.fraud-magazine.com/article.aspx?id=583.

Chang, Alvin. "4 Ways the Lottery Preys on the Poor." *Vox*. January 13, 2016. https://www.vox.com/identities/2016/1/13/10763268/lottery-poor-prey.

Cherry, Kendra. "What Was the Little Albert Experiment?" *Verywell Mind*. September 27, 2018. https://www.verywellmind.com/the-little-albert-experiment-2794994.

Clark, Fred. "State Lotteries and Truth in Advertising." *Slacktivist.* November 14, 2014. https://www.patheos.com/blogs/slacktivist/2014/11/14/state-lotteries-and-truth-in-advertising/.

Clark, Lesley, and David Lightman. "Evangelicals Slammed Bill Clinton's Sexual Misconduct. So Why Does Trump Get a Pass?" *McClatchyDC Bureau.* October 12, 2016. https://www.mcclatchydc.com/news/politics-government/election/article107819532.html.

Clott, Andrew. "The Predatory Nature of State Lotteries." *Loyola Consumer Law Review* 28, no. 1 (2015), 137-157. https://lawecommons.luc.edu/lclr/vol28/iss1/5/.

Consumer Federation of America (CFA) and the Financial Planning Association (FPA). "How Americans View Personal Wealth vs. How Financial Planners View This Wealth." News release, January 9, 2006. Consumer Federation of America. https://consumerfed.org/pdfs/Financial_Planners_Study011006.pdf.

Dator, James. "A Comprehensive Timeline of the Larry Nassar Case." *SBNation.* January 16, 2019. https://www.sbnation.com/2018/1/19/16900674/larry-nassar-abuse-timeline-usa-gymnastics-michigan-state.

Davis, William P. "'Enemy of the People': Trump Breaks Out This Phrase During Moments of Peak Criticism." *The New York Times.* July 20, 2018. https://www.nytimes.com/2018/07/19/business/media/trump-media-enemy-of-the-people.html.

Dessem, Matthew. "Florida Shooting Survivor Emma Gonzalez to Trump: 'We Call BS.'" *Slate.* February 17, 2018. https://slate.com/news-and-politics/2018/02/florida-shooting-survivor-emma-gonzalez-to-trump-we-call-bs.html.

Edsall, Thomas B. "Conservatives Vs. Liberals: More Than Politics." *HuffPost.* December 6, 2017. https://www.huffingtonpost.com/thomas-b-edsall/conservatives-vs-liberals_b_1262309.html.

Entezami, Pouya, David A. Fox, Philip J. Clapham, and Kevin C. Chung. "Historical Perspective on the Etiology of Rheumatoid Arthritis."

PubMed Central (PMC). February 1, 2012. https://www.ncbi.nlm.nih. gov/pmc/articles/PMC3119866/.

Ernst, Douglas. "Jim Acosta Thanks Trump Supporter for Apology After Rally: 'We Had a Moment.'" *The Washington Times.* November 1, 2018. https://www.washingtontimes.com/news/2018/nov/1/jim-acosta-thanks-trump-supporter-for-apology-afte/.

Fields, Jonathan. "The Line Between Persuasion and Manipulation." *Jonathan Fields.* Accessed March 11, 2019. http://www.jonathanfields. com/the-line-between-persuasion-and-manipulation/.

Firearm Justifiable Homicides and Non-Fatal Self-Defense Gun Use: An Analysis of Federal Bureau of Investigation and National Crime Victimization Survey Data. Washington D.C.: Violence Policy Center, 2017. http:// www.vpc.org/studies/justifiable17.pdf.

Fishman, Steve. "Bernie Madoff, Free at Last." *New York Magazine.* June 6, 2010. http://nymag.com/news/crimelaw/66468/.

Foley, Ryan, Larry Fenn, and Nick Penzenstadler. "Chronicle of Agony: Gun Accidents Kill at Least 1 Kid Every Other Day." *USA TODAY.* October 14, 2016. https://www.usatoday.com/story/news/2016/10/14/ap-usa-today-gun-accidents-children/91906700/.

"Full Text: Donald Trump 2016 RNC Draft Speech Transcript." *POLITICO.* July 21, 2016. https://www.politico.com/story/2016/07/full-transcript-donald-trump-nomination-acceptance-speech-at-rnc-225974.

Gibbens, Sarah. "Are We Born Fearing Spiders and Snakes?" *National Geographic.* October 26, 2017. https://news.nationalgeographic.com/2017/10/infant-fear-phobia-science-snakes-video-spd/.

Goldman, David. "Does Powerball Really Fund Education?" *CNNMoney.* January 14, 2016. http://money.cnn.com/2016/01/13/news/powerball-education/index.html.

Greenberg, Molly. "The Neuroscience of Motivation." *Kenan-Flagler Business School, University of North Carolina at Chapel Hill.* April 28, 2016.

https://onlinemba.unc.edu/blog/neuroscience-motivation-kimberly-schaufenbuel/.

"Hillary Clinton Mocks Donald Trump's 'Very Tall,' 'Beautiful' Wall." *The Week.* March 9, 2016. http://theweek.com/speedreads/611768/hillary-clinton-mocks-donald-trumps-tall-beautiful-wall.

Hornshaw, Phil. "Bill O'Reilly Sexual Harassment Scandal: Complete Timeline of Events (Photos)." *The Wrap.* April 19, 2017. https://www.thewrap.com/bill-oreilly-sexual-harassment-scandal-timeline/.

Hutson, Matthew. "Honest Liars: Dishonest Leaders May Be Perceived as Authentic." *Salon.* October 8, 2018. https://www.salon.com/2018/10/08/honest-liars-dishonest-leaders-may-be-perceived-as-authentic_partner/.

"IN RE: Bernard L. Madoff Investment Securities LLC." *Findlaw.* Accessed March 13, 2019. https://caselaw.findlaw.com/us-2nd-circuit/1635547.html.

Isidore, Chris. "Americans Spend More on the Lottery Than on ..." *CNNMoney.* February 11, 2015. http://money.cnn.com/2015/02/11/news/companies/lottery-spending/.

Isidore, Chris. "Woman Who Sued Trump University Wants out of Case." *CNNMoney.* March 11, 2016. http://money.cnn.com/2016/03/11/news/companies/trump-university-donald-trump-tarla-makaeff/index.html.

Jones, Sarah. "Evangelicals Know Trump is a Liar. They Just Don't Care." *The New Republic.* June 8, 2017. https://newrepublic.com/minutes/143213/evangelicals-know-trump-liar-just-dont-care.

Kendall, Brent. "Trump Says Judge's Mexican Heritage Presents 'Absolute Conflict?'" *The Wall Street Journal.* June 3, 2016. https://www.wsj.com/articles/donald-trump-keeps-up-attacks-on-judge-gonzalo-curiel-1464911442.

Kertscher, Tom. "Donald Trump's Racial Comments About Hispanic Judge in Trump University Case." *PolitiFact Wisconsin.* June 8, 2016. http://www.politifact.com/wisconsin/article/2016/jun/08/donald-trumps-racial-comments-about-judge-trump-un/.

Kessler, Aaron. "Why the NRA is so Powerful on Capitol Hill, by the Numbers." *CNN*. February 23, 2018. https://www.cnn.com/2018/02/23/politics/nra-political-money-clout/index.html.

Kessler, David. *A Question of Intent: A Great American Battle with a Deadly Industry*. New York, NY: PublicAffairs, 2002.

Kessler, Glenn. "About the Fact Checker." *The Washington Post*. January 1, 2017. https://www.washingtonpost.com/news/fact-checker/about-the-fact-checker/?utm_term=.1acdf5d02f8c.

Kessler, Glenn, and Michelle Ye Hee Lee. "Fact checking Donald Trump's Presidential Announcement Speech." *The Washington Post*. June 17, 2015. https://www.washingtonpost.com/news/fact-checker/wp/2015/06/17/fact-checking-donald-trumps-presidential-announcement-speech/?utm_term=.723e8636b701.

Kim, Larry. "17 Donald Trump Quotes That Are Surprisingly Brilliant." *Inc*. August 24, 2015. https://www.inc.com/larry-kim/21-brilliant-quotes-from-the-donald-trump.html.

King, Gilbert. "The Smoothest Con Man That Ever Lived." *Smithsonian*. August 22, 2012. https://www.smithsonianmag.com/history/the-smoothest-con-man-that-ever-lived-29861908/.

Kliesen, Kevin L. "The Economy Gets Back on Track: But Once Again Leaves Many Workers Behind." Federal Reserve Bank of St. Louis. Last modified January 1, 2004. https://www.stlouisfed.org/publications/regional-economist/january-2004/the-economy-gets-back-on-track-but-once-again-leaves-many-workers-behind.

Koerth-Baker, Maggie. "Why Humans Are Bad at Spotting Lies." *FiveThirtyEight*. September 28, 2018. https://fivethirtyeight.com/features/why-humans-are-bad-at-spotting-lies/.

Konnikova, Maria. "Trump's Lies Vs. Your Brain." *POLITICO Magazine*. January/February 2017. https://www.politico.com/magazine/story/2017/01/donald-trump-lies-liar-effect-brain-214658.

Kopan, Tal. "Trump: 'We're Going to Destroy' MS-13." *CNN.* July 28, 2017. http://www.cnn.com/2017/07/28/politics/donald-trump-ms-13/index. html.

Kurtz, Howard. "Bill O'Reilly, Producer Settle Harassment Suit." *The Washington Post.* October 29, 2004. http://www.washingtonpost.com/ wp-dyn/articles/A7578-2004Oct28.html.

Lang, Brent. "How New York Times Reporters Broke Hollywood's Biggest Sexual Harassment Story." *Variety.* Accessed March 12, 2019. https:// variety.com/2017/biz/features/new-york-times-harvey-weinstein-report-megan-twohey-jodi-kantor-1202637948/.

Lehoczky, Etelka. "Spot a Liar." *Etelka Lehoczky.* 2005. https://www. etelkawrites.com/spot-a-liar.

Levine, Timothy R., Steven A. McCornak, and Hee S. Park. "Deception Research at Michigan State University." *Michigan State University.* Accessed March 12, 2019. https://msu.edu/~levinet/deception. htm#Truth-Bias.

Lutey, Tom. "Trump: 'We're Going to Win so Much, You're Going to Be so Sick and Tired of Winning.'" *Billings Gazette.* May 26, 2016. https:// billingsgazette.com/news/state-and-regional/govt-and-politics/trump-we-re-going-to-win-so-much-you-re/article_2f346f38-37e7-5711-ae07-d1fd000f4c38.html.

Markay, Lachlan. "The NRA Just Reported Losing $55 Million in Income." *The Daily Beast.* November 27, 2018. https://www.thedailybeast.com/ the-nra-just-reported-losing-dollar55-million-in-income.

McClendon, Robert. "5-Year-Old LaPlace Girl Dies After Shooting Herself with Handgun." *NOLA.com | The Times-Picayune.* May 21, 2016. https:// www.nola.com/crime/2016/05/5-year-old_laplace_girl_dies_a.html.

McCracken, Harry. "Apple Adds an Asterisk to iPhone Ad." *Technologizer.* September 25, 2008. http://www.technologizer.com/2008/09/25/apple-adds-an-asterisk-to-iphone-ad/.

"Mexicans in Mexico City Talk Trump, Hillary and Border Wall - But Not the One You're Thinking of." *OC Weekly*. October 10, 2016. https://ocweekly.com/mexicans-in-mexico-city-talk-trump-hillary-and-border-wall-but-not-the-one-youre-thinking-of-7554688/.

Molloy, Mark. "Donald Trump has Awkward Exchange with Reporter over False Election Claim." *The Telegraph*. February 18, 2017. https://www.telegraph.co.uk/news/2017/02/17/donald-trump-has-awkward-exchange-reporter-false-election-claim/.

Moniuszko, Sara M., and Kara Kelly. "Harvey Weinstein Scandal: A Complete List of the 87 Accusers." *USA TODAY*. October 27, 2017. https://www.usatoday.com/story/life/people/2017/10/27/weinstein-scandal-complete-list-accusers/804663001/.

"Narcissistic Personality Disorder - Symptoms and Causes." *Mayo Clinic*. Last modified November 18, 2017. https://www.mayoclinic.org/diseases-conditions/narcissistic-personality-disorder/symptoms-causes/syc-20366662.

Navarro, Joe. "'Believe Me' What to Make of This Often-Used Phrase?" *Psychology Today*. August 31, 2017. https://www.psychologytoday.com/blog/spycatcher/201708/believe-me.

Nyren, Erin. "Bill O'Reilly's Most Shocking Quotes: The Hoodie, ACLU Terrorists and Victim-Blaming." *Variety*. April 19, 2017. https://variety.com/2017/tv/news/bill-oreilly-wildest-quotes-1202390457/.

Parker, Kim, Julilana M. Horowitz, Ruth Igielnik, Baxter Oliphant, and Anna Brown. "Guns in America: Attitudes and Experiences of Americans." *Pew Research Center*. June 22, 2017. http://www.pewsocialtrends.org/2017/06/22/americas-complex-relationship-with-guns/.

Qiu, Linda. "Is Donald Trump's 'Art of the Deal' the Best-Selling Business Book of All Time?" *PolitiFact*. July 6, 2015. http://www.politifact.com/truth-o-meter/statements/2015/jul/06/donald-trump/donald-trumps-art-deal-best-selling-business-book-/.

Rahman, Nazneen. "Avoiding Confirmation Bias in Genetic Medicine." *The Transforming Genetic Medicine Initiative (TGMI)*. January 12, 2018.

https://www.thetgmi.org/genetics/avoiding-confirmation-bias-genetic-medicine/.

Ramsland, Katherine. "Addicted to Lies: Reflex Fraud Explains the Enigma of Casey Anthony." *Psychology Today.* February 1, 2012. https://www.psychologytoday.com/us/blog/shadow-boxing/201202/addicted-lies.

Robertson, Lori, and Robert Farley. "The Facts on Crowd Size." *FactCheck.org.* January 24, 2017. http://www.factcheck.org/2017/01/the-facts-on-crowd-size/.

Samuels, Martin. Interview by Ira Flatow. "Scared to Death…Literally." *Talk of the Nation.* National Public Radio. October 26, 2012. https://www.npr.org/2012/10/26/163712863/scared-to-death-literally

Sanders, Sarah, Steven Mnuchin and H.R. McMaster. "Press Briefing by Press Secretary Sarah Sanders, Treasury Secretary Steven Mnuchin, and National Security Advisor H.R. McMaster." *The White House,* July 31, 2017. https://www.whitehouse.gov/briefings-statements/press-briefing-press-secretary-sarah-sanders-treasury-secretary-steven-mnuchin-national-security-advisor-h-r-mcmaster-073117/.

Schafer, Jack. "Truth Bias: A Psychological Cloak for Deception." *Psychology Today.* June 26, 2013. https://www.psychologytoday.com/blog/let-their-words-do-the-talking/201306/truth-bias.

Selk, Avi. "'Rapist!' She Yelled at a Hispanic Man. 'She's Quoting the President,' He Thought." *The Washington Post.* June 26, 2018. https://www.washingtonpost.com/news/post-nation/wp/2018/06/26/rapist-she-yelled-at-a-hispanic-man-shes-quoting-the-president-he-thought/.

Serota, Kim B., and Timothy R. Levine. "A Few Prolific Liars: Variation in the Prevalence of Lying." *Journal of Language and Social Psychology* 34, no. 2 (2014), 138-157. doi:10.1177/0261927x14528804.

Shephard, Alex. "Art of the Steal: How Trump Boosted his Book Sales and Gamed the New York Times Best-Seller List." *The New Republic.* September 18, 2017. https://newrepublic.com/article/144541/art-steal-trump-boosted-book-sales-gamed-new-york-times-best-seller-list.

Sherwood, Harriet. "The Chosen One? The New Film That Claims Trump's Election Was an Act of God." *The Guardian.* October 3, 2018. https://www.theguardian.com/us-news/2018/oct/03/the-trump-prophecy-film-god-election-mark-taylor.

Smith, Emily. "Harvey Weinstein Gives First Interview After Shocking Sex Harassment Claims." *Page Six.* October 5, 2017. https://pagesix.com/2017/10/05/harvey-weinstein-gives-first-interview-after-shocking-sex-harassment-claims/.

Smith, Graham, and Javier E. David. "Trump Launches Another Attack on the Media, Says Press Are 'Dangerous and Sick' and Can 'Cause War.'" *CNBC.* August 5, 2018. https://www.cnbc.com/2018/08/05/trump-steps-up-his-media-feud-saying-press-are-dangerous-and-sick.html.

Smoyer, Divonne, Kimberly Chow, and Kelley Chittenden. "State Attorneys General Zero in on Elder Abuse, Health Services Industry Practices." *Lexology.* April 24, 2018. https://www.lexology.com/library/detail.aspx?g=0eaa29c5-400d-4d36-8963-8c489b90c200.

Spicer, Sean. "Transcript of White House Press Secretary Statement to the Media." *POLITICO.* January 21, 2017. https://www.politico.com/story/2017/01/transcript-press-secretary-sean-spicer-media-233979.

Stein, Jeff. "Alabama Senate GOP Frontrunner: Constitution Was Written to 'Foster Christianity'" *Vox.* September 26, 2017. https://www.vox.com/policy-and-politics/2017/9/26/16365774/judge-roy-moore-us-constitution.

Stetzer, Ed, and Andrew MacDonald. "Why Evangelicals Voted Trump: Debunking the 81%." *Christianity Today.* October 18, 2018. https://www.christianitytoday.com/ct/2018/october/why-evangelicals-trump-vote-81-percent-2016-election.html.

Thompson, Derek. "Lotteries: America's $70 Billion Shame." *The Atlantic.* May 11, 2015. https://www.theatlantic.com/business/archive/2015/05/lotteries-americas-70-billion-shame/392870/.

Timmons, Heather. "Watch: A Furious Tampa Crowd Screams at the Press, Just as Trump Intended." *Quartz.* August 1, 2018. https://

qz.com/1345622/video-of-a-trump-rally-crowd-harassing-the-press-in-tampa/.

Tobacco Industry Research Committee. *A Frank Statement to Cigarette Smokers*. New York, 1954. https://www.tobaccofreekids.org/assets/factsheets/0268.pdf.

Torres, Nicole. "Most People Don't Want to Be Managers." *Harvard Business Review*. September 18, 2014. https://hbr.org/2014/09/most-people-dont-want-to-be-managers.

Tripoli, Steve. "Lotteries Take in Billions, Often Attract The Poor." *NPR*. July 16, 2014. https://www.npr.org/2014/07/16/332015825/lotteries-take-in-billions-often-attract-the-poor.

"Truth in Advertising and Marketing and Other FTC Regulations." *HG.org*. Accessed March 12, 2019. https://www.hg.org/legal-articles/truth-in-advertising-and-marketing-and-other-ftc-regulations-31217.

Trump, Donald. Interview by John Dickerson. *Face the Nation*. CBS, June 5, 2016. https://www.cbsnews.com/news/face-the-nation-transcripts-june-5-2016-trump/.

Trump, Donald, Marco Rubio, Ted Cruz, and Bernie Sanders. Interview by Chuck Todd. *Meet the Press*. NBC. February 21, 2016. https://www.nbcnews.com/meet-the-press/meet-press-february-21-2016-n523036.

Wallace, Daniel. *The Kings and Queens of Roam: A Novel*. New York, NY: Simon & Schuster, 2013.

Wasserstein, Ronald L. "A Statistician's View: What Are Your Chances of Winning the Powerball Lottery?" *HuffPost*. December 6, 2017. https://www.huffingtonpost.com/ronald-l-wasserstein/chances-of-winning-powerball-lottery_b_3288129.html.

"We Are Biologically Programmed to Take Pleasure in the Pain of Those We Envy, Shows Study into Schadenfreude." *Daily Mail Online,* October 30, 2013. https://www.dailymail.co.uk/sciencetech/article-2479069/Schadenfreude-study-finds-likely-enjoy-misfortune-envy-them.html.

"When Seeing IS Believing: Experts Find Loss of Control Leads People to Seek Order, Answers." *Kellogg School of Management, Northwestern University.* Last modified October 2, 2008. https://www.kellogg. northwestern.edu/news_articles/2008/galinskyseeingisbelieving.aspx.

"Where Does the Money Go: Good Causes." *Illinois Lottery Official Site.* Accessed March 12, 2019. https://www.illinoislottery.com/giving-back/ good-causes.

Acknowledgments

"Well, it seems to me that there are books that tell stories, and then there are books that tell truths ... The first kind, they show you life like you want it to be. With villains getting what they deserve and the hero seeing what a fool he's been and marrying the heroine and happy endings and all that ... But the second kind, they show you life more like it is ... The first kind makes you cheerful and contented, but the second kind shakes you up."
Jennifer Donnelly, A Northern Light

Over the last twenty years of fighting for the full inclusion of all people in our workplaces and in our communities, I have been astounded by how many people's stories—some that we hear and many that we may never know—infuse, inform and shape our lives every day. These stories—lived by friends and colleagues we may know or by strangers we may never meet—help us see ourselves more clearly, help us see beyond our own experiences, and help us better understand the worlds in which we live, love, play, and work. I am deeply humbled by and grateful for the people who have shared and continue to share their stories with me. It is the truth in these stories that made this book possible.

I am grateful to each person who shared their stories with me, and I hope that I have honored your stories with the care they deserve. It is not an easy thing to open your life—especially the painful memories—to a researcher. Thank you. Truly.

This book was complicated to define, difficult to write, and almost impossible to finish. Tim, this book would not be in existence if you had not continued to encourage me through the many starts and stops, the convoluted reconfigurations, and the challenges of writing a book about lying when lying and liars (and one particularly prolific liar specifically) dominate the news on a daily basis. Your vision for what was possible with this book pushed me out of my comfort zone, and I am grateful for your friendship, your guidance, and your ability to stay calm in the middle of all my crazy chaos!

To my superhero sisters, thank you thank you thank you thank you. I reached out to you when I was at my lowest point in writing this book, and you—like the superheroes that you are—got me back on track and helped me (made me?) finish. Thank you for pushing me to keep going when I needed the push, and thank you also for yelling at me to rest when I needed to stop pushing. I don't have the words (terrible predicament for writer, right?) to communicate what your support means to me, but I will do my best to keep trying to tell you every chance I get.

Caelan and Miles, I'm so proud of both of you—of who you are and what you give to the world around you every single day. You inspire me every day, and you scare the mess out of me just enough to keep me on my toes! I love you both with all my heart! Eric, thank you for always believing in me. I love you always. We are all who we are because of the family and friends who believe in us and push us to be better versions of ourselves. Thank you to all of you who kept asking when the book would be done (definite motivation to get it done!), and thank you for believing in that better version of me even when I may not always have been able to see it.

To my team at Nextions, your hard work and commitment to our mission is awesome to see. Joyce, I don't even know how to thank you for everything you've done and continue to do. You have truly been a lifeline in the middle of some serious ups and downs, and I hope that you know that I am always aware of how much I rely on you and how much you never let me down.

I am especially grateful to all of the researchers, scholars, writers, and practitioners in the fields of equality and inclusion who are collectively working to make this a better world for all of us. This work has never been easy, but it has been an especially rocky road to travel in the past few years. It's been exhausting and frustrating, but our collective work is more necessary than ever for our ability to shape our world into a place where everyone is valued. Thank you for all the work you do, especially when it's not easy to do so.

Thank you to all the readers for allowing me to have this conversation with you. I am grateful for your time and your energy.

I look forward to continuing the conversation.

All my best,

Arin

Dedicated To

caelan and miles
you inspire me
you open my mind
most importantly, you make me laugh even when nothing is funny
i love you

About the Author

Arin studied business at DePaul University's College of Commerce, attended law school at University of Southern California, and received her Ph.D. in Sociology from Northwestern University. As a researcher, a writer, an "attorney in recovery," and an advisor on leadership and inclusion to hundreds of organizations in various industries, Arin has traveled many paths in the journey of advocating for thinking smarter and leading better in our workplaces, in our communities, and in our individual lives. Her first book, *The Next IQ: The Next Level of Leadership for 21st Century Leaders,* focuses on cognitive biases in the workplace and how organizations can identify and interrupt these individual and institutional biases in order to maximize the potential of all talent in workplaces. Her second book, *One Size Never Fits All: Business Development Strategies Tailored for Women (And Most Men)*, delves into gender differences in how men and women network, lead, promote themselves, and develop business in workplaces and how organizations can better understand these differences to create environments where women can truly thrive as contributors and leaders. She has also authored a chapter on creativity, innovation, and inclusion entitled "Creating Creativity" for the Global Innovation Science Handbook, the premier resource for innovation practitioners. This latest book is a continuation of Arin's work in leadership and inclusion through the lens of liars, lying, and how lies disrupt the full inclusion in our workplaces and our lives.

Arin is currently the President of Nextions, a new way of seeing and doing leadership and inclusion. Prior to her work in consulting, Arin practiced law and served as an Adjunct Professor at Northwestern University for several years where she taught classes on law and society. She has developed and led comprehensive research studies on leadership and inclusion in topics ranging from gender equity, cultural integration and implicit bias to transformational leadership and working through generational differences. Her latest book features research on the neurology of lying and liars and how deception breaks down inclusive interactions and disrupts our abilities to gather and leverage collective intelligence.

CPSIA information can be obtained
at www.ICGtesting.com
Printed in the USA
BVHW042243130919
558409BV00001B/3/P